MYSTICAL WINGS

IT'S ALL ABOUT THE SPIRIT!

MYSTICAL WINGS

Let me be your bright shining star in life's dark night.
Help me disseminate God's love; we will complete our
mission here, and continue our eternal flight.

GILDA MIROS

authorHOUSE®

AuthorHouse™
1663 Liberty Drive
Bloomington, IN 47403
www.authorhouse.com
Phone: 1-800-839-8640

Published by AuthorHouse   06/07/2012

ISBN: 978-1-4772-1049-9 (sc)
ISBN: 978-1-4772-1104-5 (e)

Any people depicted in stock imagery provided by Thinkstock are models,
and such images are being used for illustrative purposes only.
Certain stock imagery © Thinkstock.

This book is printed on acid-free paper.

Because of the dynamic nature of the Internet, any web addresses or links
contained in this book may have changed since publication and may no longer be
valid. The views expressed in this work are solely those of the author and do not
necessarily reflect the views of the publisher, and the publisher hereby disclaims
any responsibility for them.

Cover photograph by Antonio A. Mirós
©Losseres Corporation 2012.

GILDA MIRÓS—author

Puerto Rican Gilda Mirós, has starred in film, theatre, and television in Mexico, Puerto Rico, and United States. Mirós was the first Latina Radio personality, with a daily four hour satellite show; from Miami to Los Angeles and New York City; her radio shows aired between USA, Latin America and Spain.

Narrator; audio guides, Metropolitan Museum of Art, NYC. Produced, narrated a film during the Viet Nam war, and many TV specials. Hosted, *"Puerto Rican Day, New Jersey, Parades"* English/Spanish, for TV. Columnist, lecturer, Web Radio: Poetry and Meditations, LPCDs recordings.

As entrepreneur; produced the 65 Anniversary of the Cuban Sonora Matancera with Celia Cruz and costars, at Carnegie Hall and Central Park, NYC.

Mirós was conferred a medal, by The Catholic Archdiocese of NYC; honored several times *"ACENYC"* Presented the distinguished *"Paoli"* and *"Agueybaná"* awards of Puerto Rico."

Spokesperson for both *"March of Dimes"* and *"The Eye Bank of NYC."* She dubbed for EWTN, Radio and Global TV; *"Mother Angelica Live."*

Miros published *"My Best Radio Interviews" "Celia Cruz and Sonora Matancera"* in July, 2003, *"A Portrait of Puerto Rico"* in 2005, *"Hortense and Her Happy Ducklings,"* Bilingual children's book, in 2006; coauthored with her mother Monserrate. *"Memorias De Los Espiritus y Mi Madre"* in 2009, *"Spirit Messages To My Mother"* in 2010, and *"Mystical Wings; It's All About The Spirit!,"* *"Alas Misticas; ¡Es Todo Cuestion Del Espiritu!"* 2012 soft cover—eBook. (www.gildamiros.com)

My mother, Monserrate, received a precious gift from God; she had extrasensory perception. Mom was a clairvoyant; one who hears, and sees the spirits clearly; since childhood, she heard spirits.

My dear mother was also a trance medium; this faculty allows the medium to receive a spirit, or a disembodied entity which communicates with human beings, through the medium.

We all have loving relatives, protective spirits; that approach us; caring and influencing thoughts. Many people reject those ideas as fantasies; fabrications of the imagination; thank God, there are many others, who recognize, with great love, gratitude, and joy, that spiritual murmurs enter through an open window to infinity.

I'm not a medium; although we are all mediums in some form; but consider myself an intuitive, or a channeler; receiving telepathic messages from the astral realm, with the assistance of spiritual guides and God's Benevolence. Affinity, great faith, and love amongst all; allows me to receive the messages from spirits. Mother's love and extraordinary capabilities enabled a close relationship with many enlightened spirits; we shared memorable experiences; learning, publishing, and helping me to correct past faults.

In the past, I was told by loving spiritual entities that I was being prepared for meaningful projects to benefit humanity, through my books.

Those sessions and spirit chronicles are in my previous books; below examples of their predictions.

Albert's spirit: *(My husband in previous lifetimes.)*

Gilda, you are a soul with many blessings. You've done much good and will continue to do so.

When Monserrate departs I am sure that you we will feel and see us; who knows if we can communicate, but we must wait for the perfect moment to do what is called a great task. It would be splendid that you could receive us; carrying the message loudly to the world.

Helena's spirit: *(My sister in previous lifetimes)*

I wanted you to know that sometimes you receive telepathic messages from Monserrate; when she cannot call you, or move; so she tells you with her thoughts, and you receive them; meaning that you are educating your mind for your good, and for the spirits work; unknowingly, you're acquiring the sensitivity to feel us.

One day soon we will begin our notebook; I'm going to create a method to dictate stories, and lifetimes to you; it's a beautiful thing.

In the morning do a short prayer, so as to establish a communication of solid ideas; a telepathic line.

May God always enlighten you, and may there always be peace on earth.

This is what happened: during six months I had been working on the preproduction of an audio book about the musical history of Puerto Rico and its performers, but suddenly in July of 2011, and out of the blue, I decided to compile a new book based on my previous works with the spirits; so quickly I left the audio project, and went on to write the following introduction for my book:

We lead a fast life style; wanting everything easy and quickly, getting to the bottom line, as soon as possible. We are an easily distracted, not wanting to be inconvenienced society; spiritually inclined, but actually physically tied down.

I published: *"MEMORIAS DE LOS ESPIRITUS Y MI MADRE" 512, pages, and "SPIRITS MESSAGES TO MY MOTHER," 428 pages;* but finally realized that very few people have the time, or disposition, to read so many pages; still, I wanted to rescue the messages; not wanting to forsake them.

Giving it much thought; I decided to write an easy to read, shorter book; taking some of the beautiful and wise messages from our friends the spirits, in my previous books, and adding the new messages that I received intuitively from them, since my mother's departure.

Obviously the spirits had their own long term plan, because immediately after my mother passed away in 2006, at age 90; I devoted myself timidly to meditation and prayer, trying to channel messages; and thank God, we achieved it.

You'll see how everything that happened has been divine intervention, coordinated by enlightened entities. I noticed many manifestations directing me towards a goal that was unknown to me, and all my intentions regarding the compilation of the little book changed quickly. While writing the introduction; I received the following message:

August 19, 2011

(Intuition from an unknown spirit.)

Yes, this is the way; everything starts slowly but there are possibilities to improve quickly; you will see. As you know this is not a coincidence; you are being made aware of many details guiding you; showing you the way.

Peace in your heart and soul sister, the miracle of faith makes incredible things happen. Having faith is to love; to love God, to love life and to love thy neighbor. Many chores are before you; select them wisely and continue with your projects. Stay calm; do not let a word or action sidetrack you.

(Intuition from my sister Helena's spirit.)

Beloved sister, it's me, Helena; see! You did it! I am ready to write, also Monserrate and Albert; we are all ready to contribute. God has made us very happy by granting our wish. We must develop a plan; I will inspire you.

(Quickly I dug up my old files, from 2006 to 2011; during that time span; the spirits invited me to write: "Memorias," (First book) and then; "Spirit Messages." (Translated book) They sustained my spirit up; eager to complete my mission; while enduring mundane difficulties which weakened my commitments.)

I've chosen the most relevant older messages; and the ones after, August 19, 2011; assuming that finally, the messages from their astral world, would be available to many souls; in shorter versions.

Our spiritual brothers, assure us that there is much more than the eyes can see; that death does not exist; it's only a transition to a better and real life.

(My sister in spirit Helena, bestowed an introduction to this book.)

"Our souls are united by an unwavering golden thread of love; a thread God weaves, and bequeaths, when our soul is created. Changing dimensions the spirit takes its bright and loving fabric that will accompany it forever.

Embedded there; the treasures of the soul; all that's beautiful from our multiple incarnations; with it, we are protected against the cold of disaffection; it is our blessed ethereal blanket.

We must all engage in working for the good of others; it is a sacred goal. Many falter and need a spiritual tonic, vital energy; thus it will be our book, a spiritual reminder; our gift to the world.

Our spirit guides say; take a pause, look closely at your life, and look at your soul, and to our Creator. Search for the light, feeling the love, peace and harmony; so as to progress and be happy."

"Mystical Wings" the title; is from a beautiful inspiration by Monserrate.

Mystical Wings

We find ourselves aligned, crossing a passive path; silent but with God's excitement. His divine site is unique, transparent, but solid at the same time; it's impregnated with lineage fragrances and scents; offering the tired traveler a majestic courtyard for rest, meditation and prayer.

We are strong solid roots of eternal sap, with a great purpose; to progress, grow, and to continue up the slope without looking backwards, without even stopping. United we will achieve it, because we're going to travel on the path where there is luminosity, love, and a peaceful force. We see a diaphanous and clear immensity of clouds guiding us.

We will achieve our goals with the brilliance of the moon and of the sea that strolls, sunny, graceful, smiling and at times agitated, we will wrap ourselves in its sway and in its musical cords as crystal that chimes and shines; with an eagerness to refresh, and inebriate. In its delirium to celebrate, it is wild and quiet, with only one creed, God; the source of all Power and Intelligence in the Universe.

Thank you Supreme Intelligence, for giving us your tenderness and the stable force of spiritual conquest. We are dear brothers of past epochs and the present. We will all sway with the fragrance of humid grass, and again we will begin to sow and to harvest; with the love of our Creator.

Young Monserrate wrote an introduction, while thinking of finishing a book someday. I found the page, after she had passed, and used it in my books.

My Blue Book   1963

Monserrate;

Dear ones; this is the fruit of an abundant crop from the garden of my life; of the visible, and of the invisible worlds. God was compassionate granting us the opportunity of finding each other again in this lifetime.

I invite my brothers/sisters, to drink this small glass of water in the form of a book; it will quench your spiritual thirst. Believers, nonbelievers, skeptics, let's all work together; marching on; expecting miraculous benevolent changes in our lives, if you have an inkling of faith; knowing that God, Divine Consciousness; is felt in all creation, in all eternity.

Beloved entities in the spirit realm, the true world of the living; I dedicate this book from my soul to you; you inspired, sustained, encouraged, and stimulated me to write these humble, definitely not eloquent lines, but, with great love and devotion to God.

His peace reigns within you, altruistic souls; His abundant tree of peace will give us all shade. There is nothing better than rejoicing oneself; while holding on to that divine emotion of peace, and tranquility, that are strong and eternal celestial bonds.

When you search and meditate, you can make a bouquet of flowers with the only and pure perfume that comes from God. Kindness and love are poems of the soul; all our divine sentiments trespass; just like faith does; they are *"Mystical Wings."*

They're durable; allowing us to fly to God. Love, love, and love; it's a state of happiness and self-complacency; I'm lifting up like the swallows.

(Let's return to my previous book; it validates my mother's absolute peace.)
Protective Spirit:

Dear Monserrate said to a soul nearby; *"I know that I have to go. I don't know if it's tomorrow or the day after; maybe next week, or in a month; only God knows when." (A month later.) "When I leave; I want to go light, light; without baggage, buoyant; that I may raise my wings and fly."*

It's marvelous to be able say that; weightless, not heavy; buoyant to fly; like the good souls. I leave you thoughts of peace and love.

Monserrate received messages from what is called the beyond, an astral realm. Born to a strict religious family, her desire to share nontraditional, inspiring, spirit messages; was almost impossible; finally, revealing this marvelous gift from God in later years. These meaningful and loving messages from progressed spirits continued, until she crossed over.

It makes us very happy to publish the words of wisdom, which the disembodied entities, transmitted in a spontaneous and simple language; filling our souls with hope, faith, shared love, which is charity; joy, spiritual progress, harmony, and peace to all.

Enlightened entities assure that Consciousness is the one, and only, true vehicle in the Universe, and that it survives the body at physical death.

Monserrate now in the spirit world; which is the real world; says: *"I know I was not worthy of His tender love; He gave me peace within my soul, and just one task to do; to share His love with you."*

"We hope to arouse your expansiveness of soul; pausing to be more sensitive; so perceptive that you can feel the petal of a rose grazing your cheek, or the kiss of a snowflake. You can hear many beautiful things when you respect the silence of your own feelings. The spirits affirm that to change our world we must change our thoughts; however you must believe it."

The day my mother crossed over, was the first day of spring; her favorite season of the year. Her last words to us, while lying in her bed at home, and aware that she was departing, are very significant, and they confirm the purpose and message of all my books; God, love, faith, hope, charity and eternal life.

I held her face and asked, *"What do you feel? "Joy"* she said. I then asked: *"Are you afraid?"* She responded in a serene and loving tone: *"Of what?"* She closed her eyes and left her body.

(I find very interesting the following description by my mother; while in trance.)

Monserrate:

I feel weightless, serene, at peace; it's so pleasant; with a sensation of relief and somnolence. Hearing low voices in the distance, approaching; it's like listening to a low telephone voice and gradually raising the volume; but not always remembering what was said. I can see silhouettes: slow, and swift at times, without distinguishing their features. Other times the figures are vaporous or seem solid.

Suddenly I feel my head expanding, getting larger and at certain moments divided, but I'm not afraid, feeling protected; unafraid. I am frequently transported to a lovely place, with flowers and very beautiful valleys, rivers, lakes, there is always peace, stillness and harmony. I see a great deal of divine lush foliage that I enjoy immensely.

For example; today, I saw a stepladder on a hillside, and I thought: "That must be the hand of God, because man doesn't build a stepladder on a mountainside. Approaching the mountain, I saw the definite form of a ladder, with details; I said: "I want to go over there; to climb it; and I'm going to achieve it." "But the steps are too steep; what if I stagger, and fall?" I answered myself. "No, no, I have a good hand railing, the best; and very powerful too; and I will not fall". I heard a voice: "Sister, it is because you have the ability to do many things. You constructed the stepladder for the others to climb."

They are inexplicable, marvelous things, blessed by God."

Losing my mother; who was my best friend, was extremely heartbreaking; my unwavering faith in God and the spirits, saved me from depression. I began quickly my daily prayers, and thank God established telepathic communication; like the spirits predicted.

March 22, 2006.

We had a simple ceremony for Monserrate's spirit; dispersing her ashes and a bouquet of flowers into the sea. My sons and brother went back home.

Going to the home that I had shared with mom for many years, I felt sad and restless, but found the right place to pray, her chair. I couldn't stop thinking about her need for oxygen; struggling to breathe.

Asking for assistance from the spirits, and much calmer, I lit a candle, placed a glass of clear water, lit incense and positioned my hand with a pen on a sheet of paper, trying to meditate; although crying; but remembering what my sister in spirit, Helena, said: *"Dear sister, in the future I will write through you; you're going to feel me always; until you are in this world of the spirits."*

I immediately thought about what my mother had also told me, a few years back:

"Surpass everything while lifting in spirit: floating in ecstasy. We must have faith, hope, and not let sorrow destroy us; overcome with peace all your situations. Feel the beauty of what is called harmony; creating happiness that lasts and endures.

You have freedom because of your faith, thus feeling agile and capable; lifted with God's Universal Energy; exceeding all of life's miseries.

Daughter, repeat after me: now I'm going to meditate; at this time I'm going to surrender myself to God. Loosen up, get comfortable, enjoy it; let a healthy feeling invade you; these are life's divine moments. You need spiritual posture; a unique atmosphere, then nothing interferes."

Following her advice, I got comfortable; feeling that I had a message from my sister Helena's spirit, so I wrote:

(Intuition from my sister Helena's spirit.)

God's peace is present, with you; Monserrate is resting peacefully; many came to give her a hand; she feels blissful. You and all of us, will continue our spiritual work honoring her, and in God's name. We all assisted her while going from one world to another; she did not suffer.

March 23, 2006.

(Intuition from my sister Helena's spirit.)

Peace and love dearest sister; there are many thoughts and emotions within you; calm down so you may become a better receiver of our messages. Much discipline will be asked from you to be able to achieve good communication. Monserrate no longer suffers pain; think that she can walk, and doesn't need pills; it was a celebration, joy!

March 24, 2006.

(Intuition from my sister Helena's spirit.)

Peace and love sister; you all still have missions to complete. If you wish to speak to Monserrate, talk, she hears you; very soon she may communicate in one way or another.

Monserrate is very happy, feeling buoyant and entertained by God's beauty. She left that heavy wrapper, *(Body)* be happy for her.

(I went to bed early and at dawn was awoken by my mother's gently voice in my ear: "Gilda.")

March 25, 2006.

(Intuition from my sister Helena's spirit.)

Sister, God is Merciful, Loving, and Powerful; don't doubt it; she is still alive, with a divine joy. The one that was your mother and your daughter, *(in previous lifetimes.)* is here with us. Her presence will be felt by you, like mine is, believe it. The enormous love that unites us is eternal.

March 26, 2006.

(Intuition from my sister Helena's spirit)

Dearest Gilda, feeling free of guilt, and knowing that you have fulfilled your duties; are the treasures of any world. Monserrate gives thanks; for your care, love, your prayers and the flowers; she says: *"Thanks to my dear God. I love you all, so, so, very much, I will accompany you always; we'll talk."*

Your beloved Albert *(My husband in past lives.)* will communicate soon; we're distributing tasks; expect it. He loves and cares for us; he is our protector; yes, a guide.

March 27, 2006.

(Intuition from my sister Helena's spirit.)

Serenity sister, peace and love; don't cry so much, Monserrate is delighted; she must rest because of her physical discomfort the last days of her mortal life. She is awake and joyous. It is the happiness of a job well done; of giving all her love and receiving much in return.

She loves and misses speaking to you all, but that will come in time. We are taking care of her, watching and guiding her; it has been a team effort. Monserrate, gives thanks.

March 28, 2006.

(Intuition from my sister Helena's spirit.)

Preach with your example; true faith is solid, it doesn't shake or crumble:

Monserrate was semi-asleep, when the end was approaching; she was at peace, a great peace. The shaking irregular movements of the failing body were not her; thank God that all her love ones came to receive her; cuddling, embracing and swaying her.

It's natural that you miss her; you were two souls bonded by great love and affinity. Our beloved Monserrate is fine, she must rest; it was an arduous task; she was exhausted, very tired. She loves you as we do and says: *"Thank you Gilda for loving me."*

April 2, 2006.

(Intuition from my sister Helena's spirit.)

Hello sister dearest, we're here; next to you; believe it, feel it, like always, now with Monserrate; she is well, still a little weak, but glad, peaceful.

You do not want earthly life, that's why you cry; longing for what they call beyond; which is our true home in the Universe; from there we take care, and watch over all of you. God is Benevolent; loves us.

(Intuition from my mother Monserrate's spirit; first message since departing.)

Don't cry for me, my daughter; I'm fine and have much to do; it is so beautiful here.

April 6, 2006.
(Intuition from my sister Helena's spirit.)

Sister dearest, it's good that today you didn't cry; waking up encouraged. Thanks for following advice and for loving us, as we all love you; you're always in our agenda.

What a blessing to remember a mother with love and gratitude; many don't even have that; they are the true orphans of that world. Your mother's tender memory drives you, fills you up; taking flight, getting up, fulfilling missions. Our thoughts are intertwined, in love and understanding.

(Intuition from my mother Monserrate's spirit.)

Yes, my child I am here with Helena, Albert, and other love ones; many more that you don't know yet, or remember; all loving you, and thankful for the care you gave me, I also want to be with you like before. Tell the boys and Nel that I love them.

April 10, 2006.
(Intuition from my sister Helena's spirit)

Dearest sister I know how much you love us, and we understand you're sorrow with Monserrate's absence, but stay calm; keep your faith as you've always done. Let life continue serenely; everything will be resolved, believe me.

Monserrate isn't alone but well accompanied, and very aware of her worth; she was a marvelous medium, God bless her.

(Mother's Day; my son Karym arrived from New York just to spend it with me. He said that I winked and moved my head in approval, but I wasn't aware of any of that.)

April 20, 2006.

(Intuition from my sister Helena's spirit.)

We are all one; a single essence united with our Father; bonded by pure love: brotherly, everlasting.

Today's a month since our beloved Monserrate, left her physical body to become pure essence; like a good perfume. A difficult month due to physical separation; difficult, with adjustments so necessary when an entity is stripped of a heavy weight; *(Body)* A lovely month of joyful awakening, of seeing things as they really are.

A month of recounting and amorous encounters; Monserrate had many expecting her with great love. She is dearly loved and also pampered by everyone; a happy blonde little girl, who laughs, as she runs with her hair loose, and her hands moving like birds.

(Intuition from my mother Monserrate's spirit.)

My daughter, I love you all. Leaving your world I saw myself among lush trees and a breeze caressed and swayed me; it was a spiritual cradle. The sun warmed me and there was an angel rocking me. Helena, Alberto, and our spiritual family were there.

I fell asleep and stayed. What you saw, the body searching for air, get it out if your mind, throw it away, it was not me; it was a dysfunctional body. I love you my daughter; thank you Father, thank you all; blessings.

May 1, 2006.

(Intuition from my sister Helena's spirit.)

Yes, dearest sister, we can talk this way for now; it's an important process, believe me; we have a great task ahead. You see, it was possible; you received your dear mother's thoughts.

Continue your redeeming progress; we know you'll reach your goals, which are ours; helping suffering humans. Go on with your daily practice; and you will see the results.

(I remembered the first message that my sister Helena's spirit sent me in 2005.)

"Hello sister dearest, let's try today;" I must know if you receive this message; If we are successful, we'll use this method in the future to communicate, when Monserrate is not available, although she will not depart your world yet.

I feel joyful knowing that our purpose, our mission will be achieved, with the help of God. All this is necessary; it's training to prepare the organism as a receiver of messages. Sometimes tedious for being slow; but we will get results at the end, I promise you.

Remember to be comfortable, at ease, free, without ties; not cold or hot; tranquil, peaceful; it can be any time, but preferable in the morning, because your brain is calmer. Take deep breaths as if meditating; relax, listen to the birds; back straight like an antenna. Everything counts with the implementation of a system. There's great disposition among many spiritual entities to help with your goals."

May 3, 2006.

(Intuition from my sister Helena's spirit.)

Peace and love sister dearest, once more we come to congratulate you, and exalt you to continue with your work. Follow your heart, your intuition that in the past has given you good results.

This is difficult, but easy, because between all of us there is profound love, understanding and affinity.

Our thoughts come together with ease, we whisper into your ears.

Monserrate continues as happy as a little bird in God's garden; entertained with so much beauty. She loves to walk and stroll among the flowers; often accompanied by her sister Pura; the nephew Peter visits them.

Stop crying, on the contrary, you should be happy because she no longer has pain. You loved her so much, that you suffered along with her; her pain was your pain, but it's gone; her joy must be your joy. Your mother is upset when you cry, help her. She is still picking herself up, and should not be saddened; help her as you did before.

The birds by your window make you happy; they bring messages of love and happiness; attuning your spirit. I have many lovely stories to tell you! How will we do it? God in his Wisdom will give us the means to do what is best. In a short time, we will develop a work plan; do not despair, with God's help and our guides we will do it.

May 5, 2006.

(I prayed and meditated waiting for intuition but didn't receive any; thinking that the entities were not available, I suddenly received an intuition from my mother Monserrate's spirit.)

My little daughter, you are dearly loved. It was my turn today, therefore the delay to begin. I know that you miss me, wanting to see and speak to me; someday it will be, leave it to our Benevolent Father, who loves us.

I'm fine, Gilda, I am well, no more pain *"Only Joy."* Yes, our thoughts always merged, with great affinity between us. I feel absolute happiness and emotion being able to convey my thoughts to you; it is our loving means for now, and I am relieved to know that you receive them, apply, and share them with my loves. *(My sons and brother.)*

(Intuition from my sister Helena's spirit.)

Peace and love, sister dearest; yes it is true, Monserrarte was extremely enthusiastic following our instructions, and as you can see she already jumped into the water. A good student; filled with Universal Energy, enlightenment, and also filled with love and peace. You'll see everything will move along well. The changes in the book are good; you got our indications.

Your beloved is here; Albert accompanies us; he is calm and meticulous; calming you down like in past lifetimes; you were always a bustling soul.

May 7, 2006.

(Intuition from my sister Helena's spirit.)

Peace and love sister dearest. What you are thinking is true; you have progressed, but without the support of your mother in this lifetime, it would have been very sad, much more difficult. You owe her much of your spiritual progress.

Monserrate softened you, taught, and guided you; she is happy knowing it; this was her mission in part, and she fulfilled it. We all have unknown goals, but very palpable at the given time. We know of your happiness with these moments of spiritual union; as we are.

Our group has been assisting many suffering families with children; we are motivated by seeing their misery, and are ready to help and comfort them; wanting to be useful, bringing them relief; it is our goal.

Monserrate joined our mission; she has always been a good soul, for centuries and centuries. God bless her.

I'm pleased to see you getting ready for greater and better spiritual projects; that is what we are all pursuing with God's help. It's a matter of systematic perseverance. Our mission is just getting started, so continue with faith, courage and gladness. Your edited books are testimony of divine inspiration.

(Intuition from unknown spirit.)

You have been a so called *"Channeler"* for a long time; the products *(3 books then)* are tangible; this is nothing new, but you must advance. Don't waste your valuable time on trivia; focus and go on.

May 12, 2006.

(Intuition from my sister Helena's spirit.)

Sister dearest, if you pay attention to God; you can find Him in the air, in nature, in the singing of birds and even in your breath. God is in everything and everything is God. Everything has a life and everything is eternal. Look well at the beauty of a newborn, there you have seen God, and also in the smiles of all children, there you see God. I see God in you.

The silence of the souls meditating; is beautiful; they look for spiritual vitality. You are achieving one of your dreams; communication between two worlds; few succeed.

There is a good reason; faith and love amongst all, and your persistence which is huge.

Dearest Gilda stay calm, learn to relax, don't rush; look at the clouds as they glide gently, *"softly"* everything is easier if you are serene. Don't be saddened by the ignorance of others, be sad for your own. Each one seeks the light when feeling in the darkness.

(Intuition from unknown spirit.)

I am Javier; this is the first time I come to you, and I bring a loving message, from your disembodied listeners. They remember you with gratitude and also pray for your return to the radio. God only knows if it is possible, but we love and support you.

God is our Savior; our plank to safety. Hold onto to Him tightly, He will hold onto you, the same way.

May 20, 2006.

(Intuition from my sister Helena's spirit.)

Peace and love sister dearest, time flies; only the astute use it well. I must tell you that Monserrate is a professor in Botany; you didn't know this facet of her spirit.

In the past, she studied and experimented with medicinal plants; one of her big passions, that is why her great affinity for centuries, with Yamara.

(Yamara was Monserrate's guide/spirit control in her early years as a developing medium; many years.)

In a previous lifetime they worked together; it was in France; healing with the plants imported from the *"Indies"* as they were called then; in addition, sharing, cultivating and studying them on an island. Those two good spirits reunited; have useful projects for the future. Your mother is very content.

(Intuition from my mother Monserrate spirit.)

My beloved child, it is so; I'm very happy. What a surprise to know that my spirit was, and is dedicated to healing with the use of plants, it's marvelous.

Yamara is a very advanced soul, and has come to visit me. She's a grand teacher, a beautiful soul; I love her very much. She assisted us when you were children; as my guide. With her help, you initiated your career; she also helped Nel in the army and when Miroslava passed over; she helped her in spirit as she entered our family circle. We are all one big family. I have many tasks; but, I am still close.

May 24, 2006.

(Intuition from my sister Helena's spirit.)

Peace, love sister dearest; yes it's me Helena, I bring roses for all.

Monserrate has the ability to intervene among you; yesterday Karym *(son)* heard her; it was she; her love and selflessness are so great that it drives her; in time she will speak much better and I repeat, you will see her. It's a great gift for all; these are God's miracles. We're a very extensive and unified family in peace and love; each one has a goal and complies; so will you; we trust each other.

There are many good entities here; also visiting; spirits in search of prayers, consolation, mercy and love; here, they'll find it. We all give them a helping hand, guiding them towards the Powerful and Divine Light of our Creator; they wish to go there. No more pains, sorrows, nor crying, only the Glory of God.

On my part; looking for a way to have better communication and thus complete what we started with Monserrate, we have a lot to do Gilda,

The stories are beautiful and significant; worth telling; on with your task, on behalf of us.

June 22, 2006.

(Today I didn't hear the birds outside my window.)
(Intuition from my sister Helena's spirit.)

Peace and love dearest sister; the noise from the worldly atmosphere, silence the chirping of the birds, but they are there, singing. The world does not see nor hear the spirits, but they are also nearby, whispering their loving messages; a song to God.

The hustle and bustle, the noises, obscure the purest sentiments; but we must rescue them; while silently listening carefully to the intimate voices that speak of what is truly of value, what endures; love, the spirit, God.

We can learn from everything if we pay close attention; the signals are everywhere guiding us, warning, directing us. Many succumb insisting on closing their eyes and ears to God and to His messengers. Sister, your ideas are attuned, flowing with certainty; constantly receiving; a good vehicle.

(Intuition from unknown spirit.)

We hope that soon you will be able to see spiritual visions, it is a present to you, but you must be ready; not yet. Go on in peace with your studies, they are helping your soul's growth. We all send you loving thoughts of health and peace.

June 25, 2006.

(Intuition from my sister Helena's spirit.)

Peace and love sister dearest; Monserrate is very satisfied with her recent incarnation, she gave much, much, love and was reciprocated by all; she shared her love and good advice.

Many recall her; young and old, even her nurses and doctors; believers and atheists; they remember her with love and gratitude. She knows it, and rejoices; what better gift. Gilda, be happy with your work, your faith, your loves, although invisible, they are solid in their love. God bless you.

(Intuition from my mother Monserrate's spirit.)

My daughter, Helena is a great teacher; she stimulates me with her subtlety and noble feelings. Her faith is unwavering; strong as a rock, but buoyant. She is also my daughter; remember that I raised her in a previous lifetime. Our incarnations have remained intertwined numerous times by love, affinity, enthusiasm and mutual complacency.

Last night, while you copied my poet Gustavo's poems, I cried with you; they are exquisite; springing from his ancient and yet youthful soul; of a love that's centuries old, without barriers; I was moved by them. I had forgotten the writings that you rescued; my crumbled papers that you saved; now finding lovely things for the book. *(First spirit book)*

I no longer think about the inconsequential from that narrow and worldly road; now my path is very broad, spacious, sunny, fresh; God's corridors with fragrant flowers. In this world we all make great efforts to forget the materialistic chains; they're too heavy, dropping them as soon as possible; why drag them? They get in the way; get rid of the chains.

June 29, 2006.

(Intuition from my sister Helena's spirit.)

Good morning dearest sister; peace and love. It's hard for you to calm your mind; you were always like that; your anxiety propels you; learn to relax a little more. Our Creator favors us by allowing these communications of love, study and teachings. We are blessed with a beautiful union to achieve our assignments.

The stories that you have received over the years are gifts to humanity. Spirits are willing to distribute their essence, concerns, their loves and aspirations to our brothers, seeking a reason for life and spiritual peace. So important are these vintage and now new, documents; thank you for giving them a place in your life and your work. Slowly you will achieve a smoother reception; calm yourself, you're restless. It's natural because it's too much.

We as sisters, in our past incarnation in New York were bilingual; and even spoke some French, understanding a little Yiddish. Our spiritual bonds are a sound foundation for this magnificent structure that we are all erecting as a monument to God, for His Love, Compassion and Generosity. We are obliged to share our stories with the world; there are many looking to believe in the soul, in eternal life; that is our market; as they say. We all become one as we reach for the stars; God gives us wonderful moments of love and peace, while we enjoy His wonders.

July 3, 2006.

(Intuition from my sister Helena's spirit.)

Peace, love, sister dear; everything has a cause; even insignificant issues have a cause. We only have to inquire and learn to read the signs on the difficult road of incarnation. Suddenly we may feel a stronger force that we didn't know we possessed, and a firm determination takes over; maintaining our faith and purpose alive, active.

We praise our Benevolent Father for allowing us a communication, almost impossible, between two worlds; we are truly alive.

Our purposes are huge, our goals immense, and we feel ready to achieve them for the sake of our less fortunate brothers. When you have a goal, no matter in what life; it glides.

(Intuition from my mother Monserrate's spirit.)

My daughter, Helena's feelings are a strong loving force, she is very determined; that's why she managed to find, and join us in a loving exchange in the present lifetime.

Laugh daughter, don't cry, I'm truly happy, I see wonderful things and places; I've seen passages from my past lives; very beautiful, positive elements from my spiritual story, it pleases me. Yes, yes, I found my poet, Gustavo; it is a great romance, with God's blessing; be happy for me, forget my illness; I forgot it. *(On her death bed, mom saw Gustavo, her mother, sister, an angel and other friendly spirits.)*

July 17, 2006.

(Intuition from my sister Helena's spirit.)

Peace and love sister dearest, with great joy I've come to greet you; we know that you expect us with love and devotion. Albert is a good ambassador; he loved you in the past, and still loves you.

Your dear mother accompanies us with sad tasks; fighting hunger, hatred, agony, affliction; everything dire from Earth. Humans are destroying themselves with false beliefs; many innocent victims.

We sooth and inspire with our thoughts and prayers; with God's love, we can assist.

August 1, 2006.

(Something special occurred after my prayers; placing my hand on paper and meditating; feeling at peace; a pleasant sensation, serene; I felt my body lengthening; levitating, with chills and tingling in my back; tears come down my cheeks.)

(Intuition from my sister Helena's spirit.)

Yes dearest sister; that is a signal from us with God's permission, confirming that you are gradually developing your psychic aptitudes. You'll have joyful manifestations enabling charitable tasks; your faith is great; it's your stronghold. Go on with your system, you do have one; advance in harmony, don't rush.

There are so many spirits caring and praying for you; it's an army of angels and loving souls that inspire you; that is why neither the project nor you will fail, you'll have the necessary data to complete your stories. Your beloved Albert; was Alexander previously; you've shared four lifetimes.

(Intuition from my mother Monserrate's spirit.)

Little daughter, I'm here, bringing you beautiful flowers from a Universal field, it's God's garden; my sister Pura accompanied me. Yes, yes, that's your great love of yesteryear, Albert; he still calls you Malena; in Argentina you danced and loved together, and then in New York.

We're always present, although dividing our time; I accompany Helena, Albert and Gustavo. Our life is very interesting; someday we'll talk; letting you know what to find here. For the good souls it's a paradise and more; very lovely souls come and go; noble, illustrious entities with blessed purposes; there are beautiful places; there's peace, and very much love amongst all.

Beloved daughter, good mother, thank you for caring and your constant concern; I'll remember that always, and I was happy by the lake, and departed in peace, believe me. Albert says; how can he not love you; you are unique!

Daughter in your life now, you have lacked a love like Albert's; we know that, but have achieved other things, and will accomplish more, the best is yet to come. Keep working on your papers; we are always by your side; your aunt Pura is here, sending you many spirit kisses. We searched for each other; and have been relatives in many lifetimes; she's always kindhearted.

My beloved Gustavo is happy with your book. Gilda, don't falter; you will have God's help.

(Intuition from my beloved Albert's spirit.)

Beloved Malena, I'm Albert, I was also Elpidio; I have had numerous names. We've loved each other greatly, that's happiness; it is a trail of pure sacred love, but we will have other romantic encounters in a major realm, with an atmosphere of serenity, beauty and absolute happiness. God is Benevolent; always surrender to Divine Intervention; comply and wait, goodness appears in time.

Faith is the greatest, most powerful thing that we possess; with faith we can get up and continue on our way, sometimes it's scary; but knowing that God loves us, and allows us to take the reins in matters, we can resolve. With solid faith we overcome all the ills of earth life and ease our daily living.

September 26, 2006.

(Intuition my sister Helena' spirit.)

Peace and love dearest sister; Lina; *(Nickname in past life)*. Thanks for your love; yes, we also want you to see us; it's a process achieved with faith, love and perseverance; we must wait.

Those old pages that you copied contain sound advice for all times; they come from noble spirits wishing happiness for their brothers. The entities who participated are grateful; that is their legacy. Love encircles us; keeping us warm, and protected.

(Intuition from my mother Monserrate's spirit.)

Dear daughter; we are all busy and very happy to be useful, assisting many newly deceased souls, arriving constantly; babies, children and the elderly. There's so much to do here, my child.

Thank you for remembering me; we are eager to achieve a grand task through you, knowing you will not fail. Your faith and determination allow you to reach goals; it's a matter of discipline, persistence and doing it.

This world is so beautiful, Gilda; I had seen it before; do you remember? I saw it several times in trance; God has been so kind to us. Here I visit libraries studying Botany; my path is decided for the future, when God allows me; He will give me that joy; but there is still some time for that.

Don't think any more about my broken body, think of my spirit overflowing with satisfaction, and weightless. God carries me, and my brothers' cuddle me; I cannot ask for more. I am truly happy, you be happy; let God's gusts lift you, don't let the mundane affect you; it's all so fleeting.

October 7, 2006.

Waking up this morning I heard my mother's voice: *"Gilda",* immediately after I had a vision of a green album with embedded multicolored stones with white letters that said: *"My Mother's Album."*

(Intuition from unknown spirit.)

Sister, we will succeed with automatic writing, keep trying; we also want greater manifestations; our goals are the same.

(Intuition from my sister Helena's spirit.)

Peace and love sister dearest; all in time with courage, faith and calmness. You are preparing your body; serenity favors the mechanism, maintain your patience. You are reaching the end of a task and then you'll have great satisfaction for finishing it.

Our beloved mother Monserrate is a butterfly, a singing bird that flies high and far; her lightness of spirit allows all that. Her conformity in life and her generosity, love and faith, prepared her for this side. She is definitely happy; stop crying; our tears come together to become a great tear.

(Intuition from my mother Monserarte's spirit.)

My daughter, patience, your compilation is going well; I had forgotten the writings; didn't remember so much beauty in the messages; I received so much love from the spirits, they were my friends since childhood. Thank you for saving them. I don't know how they survived, they contain pure sentiment; it is God's doing. I will help you decipher them, when needed; even if busy, wherever we are, we answer the call. Yes, this morning I called you; it was me showing you my album of drawings, you saw it, you heard me; thank you Father.

October 20, 2006.

(Intuition from my sister Helena's spirit. Lake.)

Peace, love, sister dearest. Art in our lives has always been powerful, enhancing our lifetimes. We have disregarded barriers with our passion for expression in many forms. Blessed are the souls that have art in their spiritual genes; they will never be alone, nor feel the indifference of the world; they will only fly with the wings of their ideals.

This place with ducklings and space has done you a great deal of good, letting you focus on the sublime; it was necessary at this stage.

Monserrate is part of this site; lasting in your memory forever. Many will come here and go, looking for refuge and lifting their wings from earthly despair, looking for divine aspirations. The birds are chirping; *"I am happy.*

Remember that to receive our messages your mind must be quiet; practice sometimes during the day, learn to control your mind; listen to the birds; walk, stroll in the cool evening; we will accompany you; taking turns or at certain times; we do have our tasks that fill us with spiritual joy. We serve the world and our Creator; we are still learning and there are great lessons for all.

Continue your work; you're on the right track and have huge dreams; you will reach your goals. You wish to assist, and guide, with this beautiful book that is being shaped, it will be a spiritual feast for many.

Remember what Monserrate said the day of her departure, while looking at the sky; *"God is out there; that's where I will go. Love one another."* So it is.

October 22, 2006.

(Intuition from my sister Helena's spirit.)

Peace and love sister dearest; today as always we come with blessings for all, wrapped in our love; they are spiritual gifts from the Universe; a sign of affection.

Those beautiful and interesting stories that were received by Monserrate; with the help of Luz, her guide; are a testament to this exquisite and real world of the spirit. Those who doubt will understand and learn that Consciousness survives after the body is silent, when the transition occurs; there is nothing to fear, you just have to love and wait.

God in his Infinite Goodness expresses His love in everything we need, while we tread in different worlds during our evolution. There are vast areas of land, to see, to stopover; there are many options for the spirit; just by wishing, amending, learning and following the indications.

Gilda, you have a guide that protects you, and also a guardian angel, two separate entities; both caring for you with the communications; thank them and God for that love and protection. The enlighten entities are pleased to be able to help. Your task will be compensated; continue to ascend, no stopping; your torch is God, lighting your path. What I said years ago, is a miraculous reality; it's so, beautiful.

(Intuition from my mother Monserrate's spirit)

Dearest daughter, I remember your delight when you were a little girl, while I spoke and sang to you; and now you still have the same habit of listening to me, in this very special way that God has given us; Dear God, gave us the joy of staying in touch. Spirit kisses to all.

October 25, 2006.

(Intuition from unknown spirit.)

With God's Grace we greet and wish you pure, sincere and glorious blessings. I am Joseph; I was a priest; but now I am a friendly spirit that bonds with your energy and your desire to produce a blessed manifesto; yes, blessed, because it contains prayers and thoughts, praising our God; may He bless you, daughter, sister, friend; continue.

(Intuition from my sister Helena's spirit.)

Peace and love sister dearest; you will receive more messages from others and from us. Our history in Manhattan will grow *(First book.)* as well as in Argentina; they were lovely incarnations.

To be able to meet and share in two different states of Consciousness is the work of Our Creator; you don't understand the enormity of this process, only God and the enlightened entities; our brothers, higher in goodness and intellect; know how to regard this marvelous feat of the spirit.

As you continue to write, you will be engulfed by a major appreciation of the facts, and what this gift from Almighty God means. I have much to tell you, but we will have time to talk, yes we will; there will be comprehensive and more compelling ways; more elaboration; it's a matter of placing the pieces where they belong. Gilda, you've won many awards in the spirit world, and in yours; expect more honorable mentions; you'll bring about, great achievements for you, your sons, and the world; you're our delegate.

(Cried with joy; an honor.)

November 5, 2006.

(Intuition from my sister Helena's spirit.)

You see; we are improving our technical skills, I repeat; it's not easy, it is a combination of elements. You will have instructions on how to do it better; seeking, you will succeed; watch your step in the search. God is your guide, do not fear but be cautious. We are content with what you've done, with your behavior and discipline.

Many notice your radiant spirit, full of faith; it is very lovely, Gilda, very special. We are so unified, that what you feel is shared by all, that's why it's so important not to lose your patience; it affects us.

Your spiritual education is forming; you'll see an outcome from the lessons you've received and your desire to share that knowledge. You'll get the desired results; which is, that the word of God, in all its purity and justice, reaches those most in need; those who have their ground ready for sowing and are collecting seeds; divine love acorns to nourish the spirit.

(Intuition from my mother Monserrate's spirit.)

Dearest daughter, your beloved Albert will soon speak to you; he is watching over you and all of us; we are many, loving and supporting each other.

You don't know how wide-ranging, fascinating this is. I found old loves; besides Gustavo, that have brought me so many beautiful memories, emotions; eternal joys; the reunions with our love ones make us so happy.

We are all little plants; each one with their own colors, shapes and healing properties to alleviate, decorate, or simply love.

December 10, 2006.

(Intuition from my sister Helena's spirit.)

Peace and love sister dearest; I repeat that I will write well through you, do not be discouraged by the delay, we'll do it; Albert also assists in this project. With God's help everything is marching along little by little; it's a gift for us, and for the world. God allows us to venture into new paths of expression for the good of our brothers. Our spirit family history is fascinating, precious; praise God.

(Intuition from my mother Monserrate's spirit.)

Daughter dear, I can also write, you're my co-pilot; God is our great pilot, along with the guides that assist us; angels, as they are called. I love this task.

Gustavo still loves and accompanies me; what a blessing. Remember that wonderful angel sustaining me? That I saw several times? He is also very close to me here; a great protective spirit. He seems so beautiful, with gold and silver wings; it is his light, because here we do not have wings. He held me while I slept away, and helped me to wake up in peace and with full awareness. Thanks to him and to our dear God.

The pages that you copy fill me with immense joy, yes, I rejoice; because they contain so much love and faith; it's a beautiful legacy. I am very grateful, that I was able to serve; assisting with wise communications from enlightened entities, that left messages with such enormous value Dearest daughter, there is nothing better than peace; peace is light, it's illumination.

December 28, 2006.

(Intuition from my sister Helena's spirit.)

May God's peace and love encourage, and keep on driving you, to complete your work. Peace is so necessary and how little we appreciate it; the root of our existence; with it we can pray, think, work and create our own harmony, our trail of happiness that guides us and follows us.

Without peace, life is the so called hell, created by human beings. When there's peace we feel well, thus we promote peace, charity, love, indulgence and compassion; that's our task. May these virtues reach all the corners of the world. Everything good is possible and happens when opening up to goodness and love; we move forward with our lighted torches seeking and bringing peace and light to the world, it is our mission and our happiness.

We are all exposed to positive and negative; our spiritual defenses are vigilant, protecting us, keeping us concealed. With God's benevolent and loving cloak, nothing confuses us; with His harmony and love we're guided by angels of peace, all helping to fulfill our missions. We are all one; so it is.

(Intuition from my mother Monserrate's spirit.)

Dear daughter; I am always close to all of you. That recent incarnation helped me a great deal; I learned and redeemed myself with my ailments, but it passed; nothing hurts now.

Yamara, my spirit guide and control; assisted me when I was young; she returned at the end, and assists me now. We have been a loving family for centuries.

January 15, 2007.

(Intuition from my beloved Albert's spirit.)

Good morning Gilda, I love reading your notes; we approach and enjoy, while you review and copy the documents; those are important pieces of our past lives; many the result of pure love that exists between two worlds. They will be published soon, and received with the same love that you have felt, transcribing them.

Our book will be the companion of many in their days of sadness and loneliness; they will take it in their arms and give thanks to God and the entities that inspired it. We carry our virtues on the forehead; they are the tattoos of the spirit.

(Intuition from my sister Helena's spirit.)

Peace, love, sister dearest; this positive energy you feel is wonderful; it comes from the Universe and from a good brother who arrived with his love.

Gilda these messages contain commitments; actually we didn't know for sure, what would happen; doing it spontaneously, but God knew; He guided us: there was, and is, a beautiful, sublime, and useful purpose. I'm also pleasantly surprised with the extension, and power, of devotion and discipline.

We will do much good; that fills me with delight. We worked in the past; and are working together again, it's joyful; Father, thank you.

(Intuition from my mother Monserrate's spirit.)

Good daughter, it's exciting seeing your devotion with those papers containing the thoughts from our loving brothers. They will leave a trail of love in this world; what many of them wanted to do in life, they did it now, in spirit; it's something extraordinary.

The pages with flowers *(Memorias book.)* are very lovely. It's happiness to be close by, and that you can feel me! You feel us! I always knew it; what a wonderful gift from God and our guides.

January 23, 2007.

(Intuition from my sister Helena's spirit.)

Peace and love sister dearest; I am anxious to tell you that the documents in your backpack are beautiful. We are all very happy and satisfied with those messages of love and wisdom that you have saved, persevered; giving them to the world in our names as one; all for one, God.

It's hard work, but very pleasant; the tools teach us what tasks lie ahead. You will feel very glad with what's coming. The collective messages by intuition, that you receive are valid, believe it. *(Doubted ability)*

We have a schedule for you, and soon you will know more about what you sensed for the book; the design. *(While traveling by plane I noticed the clouds below, with camera at hand, I took a few photos; found them lovely; using one for the book covers.)* We all feel enormous gratitude towards God; for this communication that binds us together.

You know that your mother is happy; that she accompanies and cares for you, as she did with your career; even now she does it, as you write and copy. Don't forget that they're her inspirations, her writings; ask for assistance; she is always ready to help.

(At times not understanding a word written by mom, I asked her for assistance and she revealed the words by inspiration.)

(Intuition from my mother Monserrate's spirit.)

Dearest daughter, I could not stay behind. What a great surprise this is! We can talk and write to each other; thanks to God, Helena, Luz, *(Guide)* everyone.
January 25. 2007.

(Intuition from my sister Helena's spirit.)

God's peace for all; especially for soldiers that moan, Father place your hand over them; peace. Dearest Gilda, last night you were inspired, a good entity approached you. There is a group of brothers who accompany you, and are pleased to assist; they are your invisible collaborators; writers, editors and publishers, working together, to show you the way. Monserrate's **"Blue Book."** *(First book.)* **has** good godparents. Several entities are waiting to give you hints for the book, anxious to cooperate; masters, that love God, and our spirit work. God's Mercy gives us new opportunities to correct our lives every day; each sunrise is an opportunity and brings hope.

(Intuition from my mother Monserrate's spirit; I was feeling tired.)

The hill is steep and sometimes our steps are slow as we climb, but slowly and with determination; taking our time, shifting our weight, we eventually get to the top. We do have the best guide; God. Spirit kisses, Mom. *(Mother drew me a small flower.)*

February 7, 2007.

(Intuition from my sister Helena's spirit.)

Peace and love sister dearest; God will give you enough to finish our work; many are counting on you, it's a moral commitment which cannot be interrupted. You'll have much spiritual encouragement, vigor and magnetic force from us, to work constantly, forgetting your sorrows; focusing on what's at hand. God will say what the next step is; you will receive divine assistance to complete your life.

We all have our sorrows, doubts, and questions; but understand that we are still growing in spirit; we still need a little more, to get to a higher level.

Being a big family, we communicate rapidly with each other; reaching our sensible agreements on the issues at hand; relying and supporting each other, in this world of the spirit, and in yours. God takes us by the hand in uncertainty, and sends us assistance, as if it were; *"First aid."*

(Intuition from my beloved Albert's spirit.)

God is our compass; directing us, telling us; He has so many ways to communicate, but humans don't listen, they are enclosed in the materialistic, and therefore unhappy. How to help them? That is our commitment, to open their eyes and ears; it is our mission. May God enable us to continue working on His behalf, may our Father enlighten us, and give us the strength and perseverance to assist with our communications.

Try to assign more of your time from now on; writing with the machine; the moment of the total automatic writing cycle, is approaching.

You will simply place your fingers on the keys and they will move by themselves; always in God's name. The mind serene; undisturbed, focused on this work; not for today, but it will be soon. I love you.

March 2, 2007.

(Intuition from my sister Helena's spirit.)

Peace and love sister dearest; the birds are singing happily; content with whatever God's Mercy will give them; twitters of gratitude. Their melodies are like a cradle song, calming the spirit with their peeps; it's therapy for you. Copy them, be happy, look for simplicity, the effortless, the lovely and the peace; that's happiness. It's lovely to love, to believe in God, lovely to have hope, faith, and willingness to achieve goals.

The noble spirits assisting, celebrate with you, because their messages, their feelings, and loving words praising God, will be released in book form. It's a beautiful mission, a great reality.

It's no coincidence that you were born with this goal sister dearest, you always wanted to do it; in other lives too. Soon I will tell you some stories; I always said: *"Soon I will tell you"* I knew that you were going to receive our messages.

Monserrate was your brilliant professor; you inherited her devotion to serve promptly. We wish to share our knowledge; given that we are educators; in the past we rejoiced giving lessons. *(Sisters and tutors in previous life.)* The world wants to learn; many pray, beckon, ask for assistance. God sends angels, enlightened spirits and friends, to help.

(Intuition from my mother Monserrate's spirit.)

Beloved daughter, I'm proud that you learned; yes, and that we are so alike. Everything that you read about spirituality helps you. Each person has what they want, their hopes, and dreams; and God responds.

Our spirit world is very pretty; there are so many beautiful moments in the spirit's life, from incarnation to incarnation; it is a broad panorama sprinkled with drops of pure love. See you soon; but you still have to finish a few things.

March 23, 2007.

(Intuition from my sister Helena's spirit.)

Peace, love, dearest sister, pure love emanates from the noble and kind entities; their love grows constantly and spreads like Ivy, beautifying many courtyards. Monserrate's beautiful God fills us with love; guiding us in the darkness, steering us when we lose our way; quenching our thirst, when dry; weakened by lack of love. Everything's beautiful with faith; anything is possible when there is solid faith; that is the message; the remedy is faith.

Gilda, what unifies us is so lovely; we share our purpose with all the other entities who wish to enlighten the world. God allows our communications for that reason; we are all small lanterns illuminating the path. Your mother is very happy; but she earned that happiness with her good deeds, her love, her service to the world, and her immense faith.

(Intuition from my mother Monserrate's spirit.)

Daughter dearest, we are many that you have known; helped, and loved; we all have celebrated life, and love, many times.

Everything is beautiful; look at this great gift that God gave us. Our story is lovely; so many wonderful details. Spirit life is pretty, you don't remember, but you love being here; that's why you're nostalgic; it's true.

I must repeat that I'm proud of you; because you have my spiritual roots; you were a good daughter, and a good student. Our book will be a success, among believers, the curious, and the nonbelievers.

March 25, 2007.

(Intuition from my sister Helena's spirit.)

Peace and love sister dearest; you must keep your mind flexible in order to work with the machine. *(Automatic writing with typewriter; mind wondered.)*

We will try again tomorrow. I'm not dictating, it is a great enlightened spirit assisting us all with God's permission. Details will emerge, answering many of your questions.

Spirit life is fascinating; you'll see that threads and silk ribbons are one; love binds them together, love is the base. We look and find each other to love and for support; that's part of the joy that God gives us, it's beautiful, thank you Father.

We will continue our talks; there is much to do little sister. The orientation you asked for will come, God will send assistance, shoulder to shoulder, we will succeed; nobody can afford to fail; on the contrary, rest assured we'll overcome all obstacles. The spirits rejoice seeing their plans completed, manifested. We have made many efforts for a long time; and are happy and satisfied with the results of our pilgrimage and our communications with our brothers on earth.

The personal touches to the book with your floral photographs are lovely. Monserrate's small, pretty,

wonderful floral drawings dedicated to us are also beautiful, thank you. We are also surprised with all the events of our story; it's marvelous; *"Made in Heaven."*
March 28, 2007.

(Intuition from unknown spirit.)

Peace and love; we have more data to share with you; all necessary for you to finish the stories. Gradually we will do it this way, until your hands and our intervention stabilizes; everything is possible when there is goodwill.

With God's permission; let's begin our work; listen to this story of love and light. She was good and docile but haughty; living in opulence with her family in a great city in Spain. She was attractive, with a winning personality; also multiple talents and concerns. The young man was a sailor who lived with his family on the other side of the city. He was not wealthy, but kindhearted, decent, and noble; his name, José Ernesto.

They met on Sunday in the Square Plaza, where many congregated after the mass; looking at each other a spontaneous attraction emerged.

A week later, also on Sunday, they met again in the park; this time she took the initiative and introduced herself. The young man realized that this could become a lovely relationship. They agreed to meet again soon, and so it was.

There is no reason to cry or to be sad; these stories have a motive and reasons, that are very significant for the spirit; pieces of the living soul.

Rosalind was a young and foolish girl; smug and capricious. *"She sought after and then let go."* that was her motto. He, on the contrary was constant and faithful in his loyalty; firm in his convictions.

José Ernesto had to work, helping to support his family, so he took a post on a ship, and sailed away, but always thinking of Rosalind, who had stolen his heart.

Several years passed; finally returning from his travels, to his home in Barcelona; asking about the whereabouts of Rosalind; he was told that she had married a Frenchman and they had gone to live in Paris with a little baby. José Ernesto thought her future was sealed; thus continued sailing for two more years, finally returning home.

Arriving at his parent's home, he got the news that now Rosalind was living with relatives, because her husband had died; so he decided to look for her; and the following Sunday after mass, found her at the Plaza. The mother of two children now looked more attractive. Tomorrow we will continue.

March 29, 2007.

(Intuition from unknown spirit)

God loves and gives us so many beautiful things every day. This is a great gift for you and the world. In God name; let's continue; it was a warm, lovely autumn day; birds harmonizing their sweet songs, children singing, playing while the nanny attended.

Rosalind was on a swing in her flowery garden; dreaming of the young sailor that with a sweet and gentle tone, had greeted her. Wisely, the young widow thought something bonded them.

That was a concern; she was a widow, and in that society widows died with the deceased; it was assumed that her life had ended; she couldn't dream and much less dream of an unknown sailor suitor.

Suddenly feeling a great desire to take a ride; asking for her carriage, she took off for the square; leaving the children in the care of relatives, and the nanny. Tomorrow we will continue.

March 30, 2007.

(Intuition from unknown spirit)

We know life has many surprises; that's why we must prepare for whatever comes. Everything is possible when there is pure love and great faith that moves mountains. With our thoughts and efforts, plus divine assistance, which is always available; we can do wonderful things.

With God's permission, let's go on with the story of Rosalind and José Ernesto. Her carriage arrived at the park square, as if by coincidence; which does not exist. She saw the sailor at a distance with some friends, and told her carriage driver to pass by in front of the group, and so he did. José Ernesto saw the carriage approaching and signaled for them to stop. They shared greetings, spoke and agreed that he would go to visit, the following week.

Finally seeing each other again, was a dream; both felt the desire to embrace, turning into a tender, passionate, meaningful kiss. Friends became lovers.

What about Rosalind's situation? A widow with two children; so they decided to go to America. The children were small and would adapt, and they were healthy, strong; able to start a new life in a strange place; they thought.

The plan was executed and the small family within two months, headed for New York. Rosalind's family disowned her; she saved money and jewelry, to travel and survive in the new land. Meanwhile the sailor's family gave them moral support.

March 31, 2007.

(Intuition from unknown spirit.)

With God's permission, let us continue the story: they arrived with faith and hope, true believers; in love; eager to comply and to be happy. With friends over there, they quickly settled down, precisely in lower Manhattan.

José Ernesto was a sailor, and didn't know where to find a job, but he found work in a food store and luckily made friends with the owners. Rosalind looked after the children and weaved in their small apartment; earning to supplement the income.

Everything was going very well, but one day the unexpected happened; José Ernesto became ill, and although the owners considered him, they had to let him go. The sailor suffered from a neuromuscular disease; he was weak and slow with his movements.

The small family only had Rosalind's earnings, which were very little. She had to find a job while he stayed home with the children. We will continue tomorrow.

April 1, 2007.

(Intuition from unknown spirit.)

With God's permission, let us continue. I told you that Jose Ernesto was ill, limited to his house; he was handicap. Rosalind was agile and attractive, and had magnetism; a great personality, with good skills.

She thought of looking for work in a theatre; at that time there were many theatrical groups; it was entertainment for the masses. Luckily she got a job assisting an actress, with a small salary, but she was still weaving at home and had a good wealthy clientele. José Ernesto, at home continued to care for the children who were now older. Everything was going splendidly.

In the theatre, an actress was missing and they asked Rosalind to read the girl's lines. She did it very well and they kept her in mind for future use; coming to pass; an actress was needed and Rosalind joined the cast. We will continue tomorrow with God's help.

April 2, 2007.

(Intuition from unknown spirit.)

With God's permission, let's continue; Rosalind had the surprise of her life; t was a good role, a great start.

José Ernesto was also pleasantly surprised but a little sad, because every day his beloved wife's absence grew longer. Their home was well cared for, and the children were pleased, but the poor sick man suffered pain, loneliness; a sense of uselessness. On the other hand the play was a success and Rosalind was at ease with her acting.

The fateful day came too soon taking them by surprise. They left unexpectedly, because of a fire; first him, and then she left. Rosalind had lit a candle and fallen asleep, waking up too late; the house was made of wood, it was old, so it burned quickly.

She tried to save him, struggling to drag him out, but couldn't budge him; he was too heavy, and was immobile. Luckily that night the children were staying with friends and were spared, thank God.

The eternal lovers are together; disembodying, they sought each other, and went on together.

I was Rosalind; thank you for listening to my short story. I wish to help you with your writings. You have many friends and family in this world of the spirit. I have joined you because of great affinity; as a spirit who wants to spread God's words through the enlightened spirit's words of peace and goodwill.

I have assisted you at the beginning; others will come, dedicated hard workers, loving entities who will continue to dictate. At some point the fingers will continue by themselves on the keys. Don't panic, it's for the best; the spirit will continue the direct writing. There's a lot to say; thank you for your love, faith and devotion; goodbye, in the name of God.

April 4, 2007.

(Intuition from my sister Helena's spirit.)

Peace and love sister dearest; I know you feel at peace, with many dreams and projects; bubbling, and that is faith. You must always have hope; it's the engine of our spirit vehicle.

Uncertainties, out the window; let the breeze and fresh air come in, the chirping of the birds; all that is faith, engulfing us with a celestial melody which puts us to sleep, refreshing our spirits, tired of fighting.

You have so many fond memories of your mother, of your union and relationship of mutual support, shared love; it is beautiful, and still lingers. She's there by your side, like me; you have a full room.

The flowers adorning the book pages will delight many; messages will remain pressed into their souls; Keep working knowing that you'll publish them.

I told you! Anticipating many things. Monserrate is overjoyed, because you preserved and appreciate her old papers, sharing them. All aspects of the book are lessons for the incredulous world; God's so wise, giving us this gift of multicolored ribbons and tassels.

Stories continuously will reach you; let yourself be carried away by the benevolent, loving and noble entities that assist us; it is a family group.

April 10, 2007.

(Intuition from my sister Helena's spirit.)

Peace and love sister dearest; remain calm and happy with your life, with your aspirations, and with your efforts, for an always ascending cause. We all have to improve, that's why we are linked to this planet, to this dimension.

We always ask for light, clarity of the soul, and greater faith to share with others; we want to spread our love and faith to the whole world. The book that you're preparing is a good symbol, because it has so much affection, so much enthusiasm and faith; it is a tray of honey, a balm, a tonic for the sagging soul. We give thanks, Father.

Monserrate's legacy is beautiful; *"Hortense And Her Happy Ducklings." (Children's bilingual book; Monserrate wrote and illustrated; working until a week before departing; teaching children to wash their hands, to avoid illness.)*

She served as a vehicle; opening a door with her love, peace, faith, her devotion and her loyalty; all beautiful things.

God rewards her daily, and she's blissful; we love her. Every day we must be ready, just in case God calls us; with a heart at peace, and with a bag of good deeds; that is the first class passage, a clean conscience is the ticket for the great trip.

April 16, 2007.

(Intuition from unknown spirit.)

In the name of Almighty God, here I am; there is no way to condense certain stories because the plot is too long and of importance in its teachings; we do our utmost to simplify the data. There are so many things that I must tell you; there's much fabric to cut.

I'm not Helena; I am a brother, a partner, excited about your projects. A writer and editor, in my last incarnation; now I write love letters to my incarnated brothers; eager to share divine words, and God's essence to the world.

We spirits have our sorrows and joys; working and praying; expecting the best from God, but we must learn to wait, without despair; desperation leads to failure; stopping us from thinking clearly. Sister, simplify your life; blessings.

April 22, 2007.

(Intuition from my beloved Albert's spirit.)

Here I am, Malena; thanks to our Creator that we have the opportunity to communicate. Our vast spiritual family is more than pleased; God entrusts us very important tasks and we comply; that makes us happy. Our world is beautiful, it's great; an absolute Cosmic Vital Energy is pulling us towards infinite goodness; we often find entities wishing to learn, to serve; they are looking for support and to achieve their mission.

You know that everything has a reason; there is always a cause; find the causes of what is, and what will be. God leads us, but it is our desire, that drives us.

We are all exposed to the good and evil; our moral development is the root in our decisions, the rudder; therefore let's ask God to help us to continue to grow in understanding to reach him; to assist our brothers disoriented in the darkness of passion, to lift their spirits to the knowledge of an Almighty God.

Everything passes by in the physical world, but love doesn't pass by, wisdom does not pass, peace does not pass by, it is shared; leading us to God.

We have a blanket; a cover of Vital Energy, which not only warms us against the indifference of humanity, but also protects us, from the winter winds of negativity. Remember that love brings love, indifference brings the same. Everyone has goals; with goals there is a purpose, and a determination, that drives us, first to think, then to seek, and to do.

June 1, 2007.

(Intuition from my sister Helena's spirit.)

Peace and love sister dear; here we are! Thank you for your devotion, and commitment to our work, it's very beautiful, more than we expected. We have beautiful memories, lovely recollections, not grey, but pink. There'll be more sublime moments, we expect pleasant experiences of service, to humanity; we will enjoy God's Glories.

That is an earth world of shadows, deception, of masks; many playing roles, they hide in their roles. It is a distorted world; thus maintain a spiritual balance with harmony and peace, in order not to stumble; staying on your solid feet, like God's pillars.

Life goes on, and we are learning how to lessen it, that is the art of living; faith is the remedy, the divine compress on wounds. We suffer but in time we throw away the cargo and raise our wings climbing to God's worlds.

Together in good or bad times; we are a group of souls respecting and supporting each other. We have all shared lives, that's why we feel an immense eternal love. There are many stories combined with impressive lessons; it's wonderful because we are progressing together; climbing.

Monserrate is fine, traveling as much as she can, as she enjoyed doing in your world. Adorned, perfumed, surrounded by music and art; still a loving dreamer; we love her.

June 12, 2007.

(Intuition from my sister Helena's spirit.)

Peace and love sister dearest; go on with your willingness and determination; discipline is essential and you have it.

The daily mundane routine is an obstacle for humans sometimes, because it stalls them, swallows them up. We must make a great effort to maintain the spirit free, healthy and vibrant; that is so important; persist and you will achieve your plan.

You'll be rewarded; the personal satisfaction of fulfilling your goal, the joy of not surrendering your spirit rights; yes, spiritual entities also have rights; and free will, and freedom; very significant things. Determination, willpower, justice and the desire to fulfill, are all basic elements in the spirit stem; love, peace and faith stabilizes, harmonizes them; makes them successful. The complete compendium has to be harmonious; therefore preserve your harmony. it is the core of your identity.

Monserrate is radiant; she is hardworking and happy; you'll see how beautiful she looks, how lovely her attire, as she dances on the clouds.

(Intuition from my mother Monserrate's spirit.)

Daughter dearest, our encounters are beautiful; I feel very joyful with these talks, knowing that you learned from me, that I was your inspiration; what a bliss to be able to pass on faith to our children.

Monserrate was my name, I'm *"Happy Spirit,"* now; my soul has no sorrows, pain or heaviness; *"I am light like a cloud; light like a feather in the wind."* God's light and love are immense; we must feel tiny compared to the Supreme Intelligence.

June 13, 2007.

(Intuition from my sister Helena's spirit.)

Peace and love sister dear; it's beautiful to grow, to study, to know that we advance, that we are not the same, that we have changed; remembering the past to compare our spiritual improvement. You're another Gilda; you still have some years; to share your knowledge.

So many stories that have to be told; so many sorrows to reveal, but everything will be like the waterfall you photographed; running water, moving, taking away the negative, refreshing the stones. There are humans similar to stones, but the water reaches them, the rain refreshes them; you will do it.

We are busy; there is much to do in our spirit world, because hatred is accelerating, growing, and more, and more, souls arrive confused. It's a time of turbulence, chaos; spirits blinded by hate.

Continue with your routine; more prayers and good lessons are needed; the spirits have greater responsibilities; it's time for the truth.

All is going according to a divine plan; do your part; there are other forces at work, moving, guiding; much has to do with our thoughts and the concerns of the spirit. Nothing is accidental in relation to determining factors in life, that show us the way, they are signs; nothing is a coincidence.

There are entities, a team, working with you in this effort; thanks to all, and God. We are happy complying with our duties and assisting with yours.

(Intuition from my mother Monserrate's spirit.)

Daughter, what a marvelous book; a surprise! An enormous reward for our faith; Working on a book between two worlds; that is great! Out story is pretty; God loves us; everything will turn out beautifully; our torch is God and we will always carry it well ignited.

June 30, 2007.

(Intuition from my sister Helena's spirit.)

What's important and beautiful, is that you heard and transcribed messages from wise souls, reaching us with advice; extending their hand, to assist in our evolution; that is pure love.

God bless Pio Gabriel who's listening, happy; because you've met your commitments. You can finish your work peacefully, and then travel the world; commenting, instructing; all that is on the agenda. We're by your side; confidantes, partners and good friends, wishing you spiritual success.

Life is a privilege; to advance we must make the best of it, perform it well; it's like a play, one must learn the lines and know how to interpret the character with honesty, integrity, rhythm and grace; the art of living. There is no reason to fear tomorrow; your making your tomorrow with your today. You attract everything, the positive and the negative, each person is a magnet.

(Intuition from my mother Monserrate's spirit.)

Beloved daughter; there are bitter chapters but we do grow, therefore we should forget the somber; remember only acquiring enlightenment during that passage. We are soldiers of light, peace and love, eradicating despair, sorrow, negativity and hatred.

There's where I'm at daughter; loving, taking care and protecting all of you, but like you, I work. Gilda, you have powerful broad wings, and you can fly very high, reaching other levels with flowers in your peak; that gives me joy.

(Intuition from my beloved Albert's spirit.)

Beloved, the table is set, the day is approaching when I will take your hands, guiding them to write, as I did in a lifetime; what a happy moment for me. We will be working on a mission among many and will publish our writings in the form of small books with substance.

Remain tranquil on the narrow road, at times narrower and also painful; but suddenly it becomes wider, illuminated with the Grace of God; a light is turned on, allowing you to work. Hope for the best with your thoughts and feelings.

You outline the path with your actions; it's easy, also difficult, because it involves changing habits, sacrifices, adversity and resignation. It is a reality, it's a fact; life becomes more positive, enjoyable and bearable, and you reach your goal, whatever it may be; God is our immense beacon of light, enlightening us all equally; I love you.

July 21, 2007.

(Intuition from of my sister Helena's spirit.)

Peace and love sister dearest; we are in a hurry because a great task waits. Monserrate goes with us, also your aunt and cousin Peter. Many need our assistance; we are a large group, working together for the children.

Persist with your work; your thoughts are positive and beneficial to many; we will inspire you. God gives us energy, directing us with His love and mercy; allowing us to help; you are protected.

(Intuition from my beloved Albert's spirit.)

I'll stay with you Malena, later I'll join the others to assist in a great charitable task. They are spirits with special love and goodwill; enlightened entities. Helena, sweet Helena directs this group; you have to be very proud of her, she is a white soul; she has worked a great deal, and is very loved by our Father. Go with God dear brothers.

Malena yesterday was something special; our first formal exercise. *(My fingers slowly rose above the typewriter keys, and I felt Albert's spirit energy moving them.)* I felt at ease, and it seems to me that you also felt great joy.

God allows and helps us, to use all our faculties with our older brothers' help.

It's a lot better when you remain in peace, and harmony, because with your cooperation we can achieve our goals.

(My fingers moved once more by themselves; an entity wrote the following)

How do I write this way? It can be done! In the name of God! All is well on the front; yes, yes.

Dead? I'm not! But very much alive! God is my light! Always; John.

July 25, 2007.

(Intuition from my sister Helena's spirit.)

Peace and love sister dearest; there are many stories to tell you, some are incomplete and we want to develop them; I have promised to look for a way.

Monserrate left a wonderful creation for the world; she is the first to be surprised; she didn't know how much she had done. She says that she could've done more, but her sickly body didn't help; too much medicine clouded her mind. She doesn't need any of that now; no needles or oxygen; we know that you suffered seeing her ill, but now she is light, beautiful, young, cheerful, and her beloved Gustavo is always very close worshipping her; they are soul mates, it's beautiful.

Everything in time Gilda; God shows us the way, through inspiration, ideas germinate; divine whispers sent by the Creator.

(Intuition from my mother Monserrate's spirit.)

Yes dear daughter; I was surprised by the old and dilapidated papers; it's good to know that they contained substance. Benevolent spirits approached, accompanied, inspiring me, they were invisible divine companions. I thank them for their love and affinity with my spirit.

Life sometimes was very difficult, with the vision God bestowed on me. Major conflicts occur when seeing reality, seeing the truth in those who cheat.

Now I feel happy and satisfied with my work, and my past life. I had and still have healthy, clean thoughts; incapable of doing harm to anyone; that is the best legacy.

I no longer suffer; I'm happy, be happy too, I beg you. Carry on with your tireless march, let's continue towards the top; we are many, by your side.

(Intuition from my beloved Albert's spirit.)

God is our guide; we will do His will, fulfilling our mission. Malena, you're on track again; for a moment you got stuck in your path, with obstacles of life in your world; the routine and mundane tie us down. Lightness, peace and love to all; follow your intuition. I love you.

August 1, 2007.

(Intuition from my sister Helena's spirit.)
(Stopped channeling.)

Peace and love sister dearest; you're a spirit of limited enlightenment, we know that; but you want to illuminate the world with your contribution, and that is worthwhile. Sometimes it's impossible to achieve it properly, but we make an attempt. God reads what is in our hearts.

Gilda, follow this road, sometimes steep with ups and downs, but it is a path, and we will advance, even if it's slowly. Not everything is grey, no, there is light in the road; there are shadows, but there is clarity and a sleepy breeze. There is no reason to stop, take a pause and then take the next step.

August 6, 2007.

(Intuition from my sister Helena's spirit.)

Peace and love sister dearest; God works in our favor; He loves us, providing us with the means for our work. Gilda, you're a spoiled little girl, that is why you weep so much, but you must know that we are all here, we are aware of you, we are there and here.

What a lovely detail; flowers in the pages of the book! We did the same thing in a past life; we created a book with our drawings of flowers; this is all a beautiful reminder of our past. The book carries a wreath of good thoughts. I love all of you, greatly.

(Sisters, tutors in NYC; 19th century, we made small books by hand. The first messages book had photos of flowers.)

Our dear Albert is a guardian, caring, crying and laughing with you. He brings you precious stones from the Universe; they are drops of dew that we give you; turn them all into a booklet; *"Drops of Spiritual Dew."* for a small book.

Albert is here, tenderly embracing you with his arms of energy and peace. Be alert; good ideas and inspirations will come; the guardian angels will open their ***mystical wings*** to cover you from the rain; they are your umbrella during the stormy days.

August 15, 2007.

(Intuition from my sister Helena's spirit.)

Peace, love, sister dearest; nothing is possible without God; and with peace, the most important things in physical and spiritual life are achieved.

Everything has its own pace; a Universal law is in place; that is harmony. Discipline, restraint, order; essential elements, all basic; practice this, and you can always reach goals. Everything has a purpose, a reason, a justification; achieving much, learning, knowing our duties, and commitments to God, and to our brothers.

Sister we have a lot of talking to do, but there are few Monserrate; let's see what can be done, I'm finding out, I will guide you, wait for it. May the doors of faith open up for many, and in turn they must keep them open for others, all united for the love of God.

Gilda you're a good soldier, God's super soldier; go forward with your backpack and faith. It's time to amend, time to change patterns of life, time to throw away old habits, time to repent. To recognize good and less good, it's a time of rebirth in life, and a time to thank God, for giving us another chance to take control of our lives. Today, now, is when it must be done. Nothing's easy; it's great satisfaction knowing that we are in pursuit of goodness, the pure lightness and peace of the spirit.

August 20, 2007.

(Intuition from my sister Helena's spirit.)

Peace and love sister dearest; life takes its course, and if you think about it, now the course is good. It all starts with the thought, with the intention, and when there is peace, the spirit floats above the thorns; nothing heavy touches it; gliding in a divine sway of love and peace. There is nothing to fear, on the contrary, you're happy waiting for good results, positive things.

We all have imperfections to correct; thus here we are, for the sake of improving, and that is what God asks from us, not requiring, asking us for love.

It's beautiful to believe in God, to believe in the spirits; with faith and a purpose in life; knowing there is something that we must to do, understanding that we all have missions, and complying.

It's a matter of reasoning; knowing that the life God gave us is beautiful, that He gave us a new opportunity to redeem; taking advantage of our time.

Sister you do take good advantage of your time, and you will have the reward of the good sower who sees his harvest, brimming with fruits to share with others.

Albert is waiting for you, write; go to the machine soon; he loves you. I'm proud of you sister, we will be together soon, we are always together.

(Intuition from my mother Monserrate's spirit)

Good and dear daughter; we learn; sometimes quickly, sometimes slowly, the issue is to learn, to improve in spirit. I'm regaining my strength, as a soul that has acquired much; I have abundance in my backpack; my gratitude to God, is huge; immense.

Beloved daughter, I come and go; there are so many beautiful things; Universal, lovely; so many new experiences. Your world is grey, sad, with pain and misery; everything here is illuminated, buoyant.

I feel stronger; my brothers and guides, Helena, Albert and Gustavo; all have carried me; nurtured me with their energy and love. We all work together, we laugh, we enjoy; yes, projects we have; someday you'll be included. I feel like new, that's why you feel me closer, by your side.

Spirit life is pretty, pretty; recalling beautiful scenes; it's like a movie that you kept in your mind, in your soul, *"Forever."* Those are gifts, huge gifts from God.

Tell the boys that they're my little children, my little saints; they miss, and remember me, speaking to me, feeling me, praying with me; they are grateful. They are my beautiful flower buds, with a pleasant fragrance; I helped to cultivate them; bless them. Thank you for your love and devotion. (*Mother helped me raise my children; caring for them while I worked. They were together until the end.*).

September 1, 2007.
(Intuition from my beloved Albert.)

My beloved Malena; we do have a great plan ready to transmit stories to you; it's a blessed purpose that unifies us. We are a fraternity of spirits in the pursuit of peace on earth. Little by little we will make comments; please discern and compile them, as you often do.

All this has a greater goal; to rescue those who seek enlightenment, here and there. There are good, but confused or maimed souls, who need a caring and guiding hand. God in his Mercy has allowed us to do this project; it is the beginning of a wonderful cycle of communications.

Be consistent with the dictation, even if a few lines. Relax; focus on your faith, with the desire to serve. We will do our job; something simple, but effective, in order to obtain the necessary information without commotion or postponement. Try to keep your mind calm, free from distractions; sometimes it's not easy but it's achieved patiently and with practice.

It's a necessary channel to operate; sometimes for only a short time, but it's beneficial. In the future I'll open the session and the entity dictates its own story; we want it to be a balm for the wounds of the body, and the soul.

Our obligation with God is to fulfill, to contribute much or little; now or later, when it's appropriate, a duty amongst spirits, between brothers. The truth will shine through the dense clouds of hatred; the light will glow, illuminating the way; many are waiting to begin their work.

Tell the boys and brother, that they contribute at a distance, love travels and it goes very far.

(Published "Memorias" book; Albert's and group stories were pending.)

September 3, 2007.

(Intuition from my sister Helena's spirit.)

Peace, love, sister dearest; our book has many godparents. The stories are beautiful and touching. The message is positive; about love, understanding and loving God.

You'll know more beautiful and significant details about our previous lifetimes. How magnificent it is to know that the spirit lives on, that the soul's essence lingers, that nothing tarnishes it, nor does it end; it is wonderful.

Gilda, you're filled with love of God and dreams, that's why you don't stop, but go on and on, you are happy. We have lots to do; a period of great spiritual work is just beginning, and of rejoicing for the souls fulfilling their missions. Without hesitation, clearly, everything flowing; a stream leading us to other horizons; let yourself go.

We must learn to connect with the Universal Flow with the rhythm of the spirit; it's not easy, it requires patience; roll with it; with the gut feeling in your soul, that is God; you will reach the desired port, get to work. Your children are souls that also want to comply; with principles; it's their grandmother and mother's legacy; they know it.

(Intuition from my mother Monserrate's spirit.)

Daughter dear, everything that is happening is pretty; our sessions, your prayers, the book, all that is beautiful, a product of faith and love. We never imagined this, but God and the spirits knew it. So many made a tremendous effort to communicate their wise messages of pure love, left on sheets of paper, now converted into pages of a book; our loving bouquet for the world; thanks to our Father and brothers.

Albert is here, he also has a great strategy with you; you are an ambassador, you're our partner, it's a privilege; I am so honored that I taught you, guided you, and encouraged you; it is my great trophy.

(Intuition from my beloved Albert's spirit.)

Beloved Malena, go forward; our work continues with determination, we are concerned about helping those who moan in the swamps of life, those who feel lost in the bushes; we ask that they will find the safe path, the path to God; searching to do charity. We have the power, yes, and a healing power, like relief from God to wipe tears, and heal the wounds of the soul.

There is no falsehood in us; everything is real, a solid union, pure love given in sacrifice, during the tempest. No matter how difficult the task, there He is, He who really loves, God loves us intensely; we give thanks by accomplishing our mission; it's a sublime landscape of loving spirits. The road is illuminated, a light surrounds us, and we leave together in peace. Stay happy; delighted in the wonder that we live. We are privileged, and I am glad, and love you.

September 9, 2007.

(Intuition from my sister Helena's spirit.)

Peace and love sister dearest; there are so many things to see and to learn; the Universe is so huge; what a wide world is waiting for you, Gilda! We will all stroll together in God's gardens.

Life passes us by quickly; you know it; take advantage of every peaceful instant; search for it, I know it makes you happy; it will relieve your burden, cradle you in God's beauty. There is your hammock. *(I thought about my hammock, that I hadn't hung up.)* You will hang it! How blissful to believe in God and eternal life; there is nothing better, nothing.

September 23, 2007.

(Intuition from of my sister Helena's spirit.)

Peace, love, sister dear; nobility of heart is essential, detachment of all the materialistic, is also required to follow in God's path.

Preaching, teaching and illuminating the needy; committed to complying with this sacred task, no exemptions. Continue enthusiastically facing pitfalls, fulfilling; crushing walls of indifference; and opening doors of love with your love; that way you teach a lesson. Not postponed or disabled; on the contrary, the more resistance, the harder we push, with greater force; striking a goodwill blow of affection; thus overcoming affliction.

Life is a maze, but we learn to take breaks, to find the right path; and we find it. True, we can be desperate, but in the end, we find a way out of the maze. Everything is action, visible and invisible; everything's in motion; follow inspiration, follow life's pace; we'll speak in your ear with advice.

God will send his messengers to supervise, because your mission is valuable; perhaps your life is not, but your mission is. I I love you, we all love you. Gilda, love brings us closer to God. A flower is about to open; seeds, and flower buds; it'll be a beautiful flower with fragrance for the world; you cared for it.

(Intuition from my beloved Albert's spirit.)

God's everything; we are gardeners and have our baskets and canasta's full of delicious, healthy seeds, well-tended, which we brought from far away.

We want to irrigate and plant, giving fruit to many; there's hunger, thirst of body, and soul.

We're happy approaching, transmitting joy with our thoughts; it's a dream come true; we'll never separate; life's eternal. New roads are opening up; spacious, with a radiant sun, that's God, illuminating.

We are a large army of happy souls that march; singing in harmony to our Creator. Our hymns are of love, peace and blessings. We spray here and there, raising our voices to eternity, to the Omnipotent Sovereign Creator. You also sing with your work, and your thoughts; your acts of faith and goodwill; all this is of value. It's wonderful that you incarnated Gilda, you were born with a star; that star will shine, illuminating many as in the past; Malena, Albert Paoli loves you.

October 8, 2007.

(Intuition from my sister Helena's spirit.)

Peace and love sister dearest; everything is more than ready, we will carry on our backs a burden that will feel lightweight, not heavy, because our faith and encouragement as spirits that believe, lessens the heaviness. It's time to water the seeds that will come forth, in many gardens and orchards.

Many will be interested, some curious and some indifferent, but those wanting to be in the know, will also take a look at these flowers and delicious fruits that are offered to satisfy their thirst and hunger to love, to believe and to be charitable.

You Gilda, in a small and humble way offer a valuable service. We're happy, and more than willing to continue supporting you with your work; we know that you want results and sometimes you doubt a little of your ability; all that is to be expected. Let us take you by your hand, as the little girl you are, and lead you to an abundant lane that will make you happy. Try to keep your mind still.

We must take a trip on the wings of the Sun and the Moon, between Illuminated Stars. There you will find Vital Energy to survive, and share; brightness that's not blinding; but on the contrary, it supplies sufficient light to see clearly. These are enigmas, but in time, you will know the lessons they contain. We all have had sad and turbulent times, but we learned on our journey, we have corrected and we have won.

(Intuition from my mother Monserrate's spirit.)

Beloved daughter, gazing at the spiritual picture, I see how lovely it is! You have divine assistance, they approach you, the illuminated spirits inspire you, and they are your allies; your work with the book did you much good; it is of mutual benefit.

I remember my life with you; our struggles and victories; God always gave us His Powerful Hand; you just have to open your eyes to see His love.

My recent existence was very interesting; I did the best I could and feel comfortable; because I gave good fruits; you, my son, and grandchildren. God loves us; Albert hugs and loves you very much.

October 13, 2007.

(Intuition from unknown spirit.)

God is everything; let's march with faith and joy towards Him as grateful souls. There is a straight, lighted path; we will go into it, hand in hand, shoulder to shoulder, elbow to elbow.

His Mercy and Goodness allows us to act; we are eager to ascend by assisting others. This task is important; it's better that way, of great satisfaction to all; let's undertake this blessed match; praise God.

My name is Jorge Luis; I'm your friend, and I want to achieve now, what I could not do in my short life. I have vigor and passion and a burning desire to be useful to humanity. With the help of God and my brothers I will achieve it. For me it is a great first step; I'm one of many that are grateful, thank you; let us move forward in God's name.

(Intuition from my beloved Albert's spirit.)

God is always good, and wise; we should be available to Him with faith, and strength, to continue our blessed effort. Yes; the spirit philosophy will bring peace and relief to the suffering world.

Gilda, you are lovable; things get resolved for you; they are given to you, materializing due to your goodwill and your commitment, faith and devotion. Routine depresses you, but discipline helps you, in your daily living; not breaking down is a virtue.

Soon you will have the pleasant surprise to feel my hands working independently on yours. We are looking forward, for it to happen, and with practice it will be achieved, let's continue practicing. Thank you.

October 18, 2007.

(Intuition from my sister Helena's spirit.)

Peace and love sister dearest; we are happy, very happy because the book is taking shape. God and his messengers are always illuminating you, to reach the correct decisions. You have the inspiration of teachers allocated to this work, yes, that's it; the allocation, the task, the discipline, all that is very important to carry out this project.

Thank you Father for everything, everything, that we have experienced, and what we are living now; this is a very interesting moment, it is an act of faith, of solidarity, between worlds. Search, knock, yes, knock on doors, you'll have a response.

(Intuition from my mother Monserrate's spirit.)

Dear daughter, I have just a few minutes; I'm in a hurry because there is so much to do here; there is great sadness, sorrow, necessity. I have a big task and I am happy to fully comply.

Our love is eternal, durable, strong and subtle. These are special moments for all, few are so privileged. It is an open window; we may be far, but we will always answer your call; praise God that we can do it.

(Intuition from my beloved Albert's spirit.)

Hello my love, we need illumination. God is our guide and Savior; we will do what we must do, to instruct our brothers in sorrow. Everything is going divinely; radiant roads open up in the fog of doubt. We have a large ray, a powerful, immensely large lantern, which is God.

Many of us meet here, but not imposing; asking, for time to bring our good wishes and aspirations, our divine goodness, and offerings; it is our task.

We're confident; waiting, but aware of your selflessness, your discipline and your desire to serve our God and humanity. Everything's in place, things are aligning; don't despair ever, stay calm and with great faith; so begins and ends a good deed.

What can we do? Try; keep hitting the keyboard until something happens. Submit your request to God; put it there on the table.

Let's continue these exercises that give us the skills necessary for our work. God can do anything. That is it! *(My fingers moved alone on the keyboard, writing the following.)* **God is our joy; we are overjoyed. Kiss the world with your work.**

Love, and more love; I too, love you. See, all is not entangled; with God's help there are clear, open and subtle things on the way, I would like to continue alone: *(Automatic writing)* **Love thy neighbor as thyself. We will try; we will get it; that is that!**

October 29, 2007.

(Intuition from my sister Helena's spirit.)

Peace, love, sister dearest; it's beautiful to wake up knowing that God loves us, that we are useful to the world, that our work will alleviate many; this is so true, sister. Call upon the Father for shelter and spiritual encouragement; may you all have the strength, love and vigor to continue on the path of righteousness; each fulfilling their duty, and looking for God's light; the only light that really illuminates the path to love, and goodness. We all want to comply; it is our duty as a spirit community.

Thanks to our Creator we are able to pray, love, advance, improve and progress. You will eventually be happy, but first you must perform your duty, with your beautiful books. The messengers helping are God's hands; listen to His voice, feel His breath.

November 10, 2007.

(Intuition from my sister Helena's spirit.)

Peace and love, sister dearest; may all the goodness, the positive and prosperous, reach you all. We love you so very much; we accompany, take care, worry about, and we rejoice with you. You are our roots; it is all part of the same tree, if one hurts, it hurts everyone.

May God's peace shield, and captivate us all, to continue growing. You will achieve it Gilda, because your devotion is sincere; in time you will perfect the method of automatic writing. We are ascending, accomplishing considerably; climbing steps; and the staircase is long, but there is no reason to falter, only to take little pauses, a short break and continue as climbers do.

Faith is beautiful; it's a balsam of vigor that surrounds and revitalizes; there's no better medicine. Be calm, while looking for new avenues; completing your journey to progress.

(Intuition from my mother Monserrate's spirit.)

There are happy, and also sad memories, of your love and innocence little daughter, of your eternal devotion to the spirit movement; it has been a whole lifetime of belief and faith. The noble spirits and your faith carry you; they have been your godparents, and now they are there with you; I love what I see; they are very lovely things.

Spirit life is beautiful; I brought my creations in my suitcase. God has rewarded me, because I can see your nobility, and dedication, and I know that I was a good gardener. My grandchildren are decent, they have good feelings; loving you, loving me, and expecting from God.

November 15, 2007.

(Intuition from my sister Helena's spirit.)

Peace, love, dearest sister; quietly you will have time to finish our work. Life smiles at you Gilda; take advantage of this moment; relax, let events flow.

We have told you that there is a reason for everything, and God is the only one who knows everything; we as spirits only perceive, sense or guess, putting our hope in Him, placing all our trust in His hands.

The Universe is so immense, and divine laws are so wise that our tiny brains can't conceive them, but we are learning, searching, responding, and fulfilling our tasks and our goals. God helps us always, giving us a hand or advice; assistance is always there. With this, we are telling you that whoever seeks, finds; it is as easy as that. If you move you obtain.

Sister you did the right thing by isolating yourself and harmonizing; cleaning up your patio in peace; you've planted, and will have very beautiful flowers, which are your projects for the world, they are beautiful, interesting, very enlightening and joyful.

Everything is beautiful with our thoughts placed on God. When we give ourselves to Him everything turns into beauty. Our hearts calm down, our health improves and thoughts clear up, creating the harmony necessary to alleviate, illuminating; guiding us to complete our task.

We are your partners in this task; the Universal company can be an annex; Losseres Corp. Universal, nice name! It has been a beautiful life of growth; of

suffering, yes, yes, but also of progress; and that is what it's all about. With God all is linked; it is a long string of love, a *"Chain of Love."*
(Intuition from my mother Montserrate's spirit.)
(A breeze coming through the window.)

Daughter dearest, we come as a soft puff of air through the window. God is Benevolent, allowing us to embrace each other; while in different worlds. These blessings make us happy, knowing that our arms continue linked; holding hands. Nobody gets lost; nobody falls or collapses because they are supported by our invisible arms of pure love.

I have visited many beautiful places; it is lovely, lovely, as my beloved Helena and Albert had said. Here we have assigned tasks; I am grateful and so pleased with what we can accomplish together; someday you will understand me better.

I see by your side a small white dove with a twig of an olive tree in its beak; taking a message of love, peace, goodwill and eternal life, to the bereaved, the afflicted; to those who feel heat and thirst for love.

November 23, 2007.

(Intuition from my beloved Albert's spirit.)

Peace and peace; it is the key to think, and to execute, to glide, keeping internal harmony which gives external harmony. Knowing how to think is a victory, we are slow in learning to think; we must not do anything in haste, but think, calculate and then do; asking God for illumination to make decisions. Beloved, rest; you have the ability, and with God's help, you will do a row of projects for the coming year, with great satisfaction.

Monserrate is always a guardian, taking care of all, saying: *"They are my life."* The boys remember everything about their childhood; their grandmother's tender love, respecting her memory, respecting God and the spirits. Love is beautiful, and in spirit it is heightened.

God teaches us the way, but it's up to us to follow the indications; each one feels their direction inside, it's the voice of the conscience; your soul that speaks to you; be sure to listen; to the small still voice.

We're glad seeing the efforts each one makes; correcting and helping with whatever, but it does depend on each one in the final stretch. Patience is a virtue that is developed, polished; a sign of progress. Continue with a white flag of love and peace. To the entities interacting with you, thank you. I love you.

December 1, 2007.

(Intuition from my sister Helena's spirit.)

Peace, love, sister dearest; peace is the glorious key that opens all doors. Your mother Monserrate's faculty was and is very special; she was a wonderful receiver of Universal messages. Gilda, thank you for being the way you are; your love picks you up, and transports you; you're a huge receiver of energy, of the soul of things.

Everything in life can be resolved, you just have to think, and try; even with divine assistance, we must find the means, the tools to mold our sculpture; and the image that we want to create; it depends on us, on the way that we do it. Knowing that we have God's inspiration, we must invest time, and energy. We're all artists, co-creators of our favorite picture, which is our life; but it depends on each one of us.

We have said that discipline and peace are essential ingredients for the mixture; along with the colors, which are our emotions. We can then take a step back, to see it well, and appreciate our work; and be satisfied with what we see.

Our incarnation, our life, can be beautiful and full of marvelous wonders, if we look, and learn to appreciate them. You just have to take the straight path; it may be longer; but there're no *"Short cuts."*

Sometimes we are confused; making mistakes in our desire to fulfill goals; but, let's keep our soul alert; with eyes fixed on a point, which is God's Benevolence. He lights the way, and there is no darkness, only sun, breeze and stars. He guides us; ideas come, and calmly major works are carried out.

It's good that you're always available; you're disciplined and consistent; so God blesses you and responds. We all have goals, but some humans stay off track until they realize it, and then get up again. Sometimes pauses are necessary; you've learned to sit during those breaks; that's a secret to happiness.

Sister, there is so much beauty in our world; it is indescribable, you are limited. The time will come soon, the great moment as expected, so desired by all. Thank you Father for the powerful love that binds us, for the joy of believing in Thee; for so many blessings that only with actions, we can give thanks.

(Intuition from my mother Monserrate's spirit.)

Dear daughter, loved by all of us; I can see your peace, they are pale colors, *"Pastel colors"* subtle, as I liked, and still like; there are wonderful colors here.

Gilda, you color the pages of the book and give it life with your feelings; it will be a book to review and revise. I feel great joy for the immense love that is noted by all of you, and us; the chains are thick and solid, but not heavy; on the contrary, lightweight, helping to elevate us, because one rises, picking up others; a love garland; *"Floral Wreath of Love."*

Calmness with passion; what's that? Calmness with passion, allows us to love intensely, keeping calm; which is the confidence, that we will meet that someone.

Wishing my grandchildren, happiness and health; and calmness, with passion. Thank you, good and pretty God; for so much happiness.

(Intuition from my beloved Albert's spirit.)

Peace in the world, and among brothers of goodwill; health to continue building castles, and not in the air, but on firm ground, for others to escalate; seeing God's majestic horizon. We want to offer our love with our tasks, so humans may wake up, think, and go towards our Creator.

There are many blinded or myopic souls, and others who go in a caravan blindfolded, but we have a mission; to give them light, giving them a candle or lamp, so that they may see the way; and even with bandages, they will be able to see God's fire of love. Father help us, you allowed us to congregate; we know that there is a great need to open minds and souls to the truth. The body is short-lived, however they have made golden idols of it; there is need, and we want to help.

Yours is a simple and domestic task, Malena, but with grandiose sense and purpose. You have godfathers; controls in high places and connections in heights; they can move things. We only ask for enlightenment to see the way, not to fail you Father; nor fail ourselves, but to love you, and us.

A Merry Christmas and Happy New Year; that can become a reality when you remain in harmony; forget, discard uncomfortable negative memories. Thinking only of God's blessings, moment to moment, day by day; thinking positively, the mind busy on goodness;

It is a booster, a tonic, that strengthens the spirit; then able to carry heavy packages, throwing them on your shoulders and still going uphill. The spirit that is a believer does it with God's help; without looking back, without hesitation and with a commitment to fulfill; walking forward.

There are many moments of enlightenment when working with love and goodwill; in this way the advanced spirits can approach you; a door and a window opens to God's messengers; those are the necessary conditions; that's all they ask for.

December 10, 2007.

(Intuition from my sister Helena's spirit.)

Peace, love, sister dearest; here we are, ready to establish a current with you, and the others; there are always others listening. God protects us with his love and power, believe me.

Each one has a place; we are all musicians in an extraordinary Universal orchestra. Learn to play in order to join the group; serenade the world.

May the joy in your soul, and your heart, never cease, dear sister; there are broad avenues with leafy trees, and at the end of the road there are swans and multicolored birds; listen to the singing of the birds; small and large, there is great joy.

This is your life Gilda. Don't stop, never ever; no, take breaks on the way, don't lose the Vital Energy, the divine rhythm, that accompanies you, it's in you.

By your side glide very subtle entities that carry in their strong arms, fruits, and a bountiful harvest to share.

How to assess things? What does one do when going to the spirit world? Whatever is not seen, but felt in the soul, that is the detector of worth; the soul. *"The soul detector tells you what is of true value."*
(Intuition from my mother Monserrate's spirit.)

Dear daughter, the atmosphere is much calmer. Listen to your old radio interviews; it helps you, like a tranquilizer for your soul. Remember the joy that you offered the world in your capsules of love; that was serving God. Gilda, thank God that I was able to give you a hand; that makes me so happy.

Now I come and go; like a watchman, taking my light. I'm going to New York with you tomorrow; I will stroll, I can walk, I can fly; I'm happy; *"Happy spirit."*

December 21, 2007.   *New York*
(Intuition from my sister Helena's spirit.)

Peace, love, dearest sister, everything is easier; now we are more in step; this is love and discipline in action. You must be happy because it's a lovely time, prominent; a result of planting, seeking and learning.

Because of your mother's effort, and the help of the benevolent spirits, now you think and reason; that's why you're happier, that's true; the good news is, that you've learned. The nightmare you've lived cleared your mind; purified like a baptism.

We have to see tribulations in that manner, so that we can accept them; now there is peace, and serenity in your soul. It is a memorable phase of spiritual development; you will assist many in the future with your advice, your work, and with our books; charity will be done. You will help the ones grieving; with sadness, because of the loss of loved ones. You'll see it and be glad; we're requesting a great manifestation, asking God to accomplish it; where there's a will, there is a way.

There are so many wonderful things in your life Gilda; spectacular memories, that few feel; even now we are experiencing a crystal page, like children; transparent, clear and clean. We as a spirit family are like crystal glasses, depending on the content that each one has, so we sound.

(Intuition from my beloved Albert's spirit.)

God always gives us everything; indulging us, calming, delighting and alleviating us by sending His messengers to comfort us. Many happy entities pass by, wishing you a good morning and thanking you for your love and enthusiasm in the past, and now; for helping them. You must be happy receiving divine inspiration; your windows are open and God's fresh air enters.

Love is the greatest force that exists in the Universe, it's the power that drives us, lifting us; but we must value it, knowing that we do love, and why; appreciating and tending to that love; because it's a very delicate plant that easily damages.

The sun rises every day; and so is our faith alive on a daily basis; it's an ardent and strong faith that embraces those around us, it's a faith that grows and spreads, that others perceive and are warmed by it; a faith that serves as a generator to the living dead. It's a faith that lifts the spirits of those who are asleep or drowsy. That's why we want to share our faith, and our love, with the world; that is why we are here.

Everything is ready for the next chapter of peace and prosperity; you are also ready.

The great book, in your hard working hands; lift it, and place it on a stand, when published; so all may read it; offer it to the world; sharing God's Kindness and Compassion; you'll have the great joy of seeing it sparkle.

With God's help, as promised; we will begin to tell you anecdotes, for another manual; later on. *(This book)* With beautiful, wonderful stories; I see a whole line of booklets, with inspiring messages; benevolent spirits surround them; want to contribute to the cause with stories; in the future they will do so.

You're our hands! It's beautiful when we comply with a clear conscience. The commitment is greater now; it's more serious; to complete the tasks. We will love each other eternally.

January 1, 2008.

(Intuition from my beloved Albert's spirit.)

Happy New Year dearest, loving, Malena; your spiritual growth has been slow but steady. It has been a rough road, turbulent and sad, but with great achievements and impressive progress because of your faith and your dedication; you are hardworking and determined. That is the highest reward for a spirit that wants to advance; to learn, and to share, with the world. It's so great to be eager, to wake up in the morning with determination; it's beautiful and it's acquired with faith and goodwill.

Always leaving the window open for inspiration; God sends enlightened messengers to illuminate you; that is Divine Grace; few have that gift. It's a result of a long period of love and hard work. With God's permission, I'll move your hands, to write fascinating stories.

January 5, 2008.

(Intuition from my sister Helena's spirit.)

Peace, love, sister dearest; each one has gifts and skills; each one has a task to fulfill; those are blessed assignments that we must do with love, and devotion. Our Father allows us to approach you and communicate; that is unusual in that world. It is joyful to work together for the good of humanity; that is our mission. What we did in previous lifetimes, we are doing again; lovely, lovely are our meetings. Who will believe it? It's miraculous and beautiful; it is a reward from God.

(Intuition from my mother Monserrate's spirit.)

Loving daughter and mother; yes, those are wonderful moments, while we are all creating. Many contribute; writers, artists, and editors. The creative department is led by a venerable teacher; he heads the group. Yes, soon we will feel jubilant with the birth of our creation. *(Memorias book)* Bless you all.

Yesterday I accompanied the group; I liked the changes you made to the covers. Thank you for being alert, and for following your intuition; an active sensitivity is a door that opens to infinity.

Everything moves ahead, nothing remains, it's an accelerated pace of events happening constantly. It seems like nothing is happening, but it is a parade of facts, positive, negative, indifferent.

We are all striving to improve the environment, to ease sorrows, to manifest the love of God, and to present it to the skeptics. We are assigned beautiful tasks by God. Everything in life is like that; giving and receiving.

January 16, 2008.

(Intuition from my sister Helena's spirit.)

Peace and love sister dearest; stop and think about the miracle that has happened during these years of tears. A beautiful work has been born from your sweet mother's memory, and our very special relationship. The book has nuances, dreams, hopes and illusions, but also faith and love of God. It is a compendium of God's love and charity with words for our fellow man.

It's a long road, but you're planting roses and you will have petals and rose perfume. What an immense privilege to see this successful project; it is a lovely solid chain that leads us to a better way to serve humanity.

(Intuition from my beloved Albert's spirit.)

Here I am Malena, awaiting my turn; I feel like a church bell because you are improving the book; a great aspiration for all. The pages will sing, carrying a Universal Serenade to humanity.

Interesting moments are on the way, in relation to this work; it's a springboard, a blessed suitcase, carrying you to places of spiritual delight. Forever we will be linked in pursuit of God's light; our paths will always be illuminated, because we have peace and love in our hearts.

Nobody can remove the brightness of faith and hope that is infused in your soul and face; seen by all as you pass them by. It is the fragrance that leaves your soul; healthy emissions that surround the others when encountering kind souls. Walk, brothers, walk; each one looking for the spiritual site, which goes towards God.

Sometimes obliged; we must pause, but we go on, following the path traced by our Creator. Faith, peace; are calming factors; incredibly, that stimulate; that's why we must care, and cultivate them. Don't let others obscure nor stain them; we must polish them daily, showing them off to the world; with a shortage. Go on, we are many, and are counting on you.

(Intuition from unknown spirit.)

Love in the cold hearts of the world, less hate, more love. Peace and love; that's it, and more; for all of you, who are a group of noble spirits; all branches of a large tree; *"Branches from the same tree."* That's why you love trees so much; they remind you of our spiritual family and its extensions.

God loves us just the way we are, but hopes that we will be better for our own good, for the good of our Universal brothers; our Universality is on the line.

Every day we mold our future with our thoughts; keep them pure. There is a purpose to life; we are not here by chance, definitely there is a purpose to life; we just have to find it and we usually do. That is true happiness; step by step, maybe slowly, but steady. You will feel complete happiness when you achieve your goal; your spiritual goal. God will help us in our endeavors; loving you all, now and forever.

January 20, 2008.
(Intuition from my sister Helena's spirit.)

Peace, love, sister dearest; light in the darkness, clarity of soul, to know, and to enjoy what truly is valuable; not blinded by misery or by happiness. May we see truth, reality, benevolence, and what endures eternally; at times, we foolishly search for happiness; inflexible in our assessments.

What helps you Gilda, is that your life is very private, rather isolated; your work gives you a sense of balance. The great thinkers stay away from the masses, speaking to themselves. *(I had evidence of receiving telepathic messages; that it was authentic.)*

How can we convince you, that our contact is accurate? You have seen it with your own eyes; it is real, positive proof; that it's not your imagination.
(I doubted my ability.)

Pay more attention to your thoughts, from now on because we will be sending more messages; in time it will be easier and more spontaneous, when your life and circumstances are calmer. *(My youngest son's*

difficulties affected me; my elderly father was ill and required much of my attention.)
January 21, 2008
(Intuition from my sister Helena's spirit.)

I always ask for illumination to see the steep road that leads to righteousness; learning to read the signs along the road; knowing when to stop, or to go. That's the art of living.

Praise God who gives us intellect and common sense, plus the necessary love to seek out, and be of help; discarding the nastiness that suffocates; that is the spirit learning and progressing.

Review your life; think, contemplate those stops, detours, and spirals; you'll know if you've learned. Happy the soul that looks back, seeing improvement of his wise spirit, that has goodwill, and a desire to fulfill God's wishes. Your life has been a narrow and twisted road, but now it will be wide and direct; you also have good company; we pray for all of you, and love you.

Go on in peace; go as the breeze, lively and proud of spirit, snuggled while you walk. It's a beautiful day, with sun, breeze, stillness, peace in the soul and vivacious hope. We believe in you, Father, and love you.

Carry on with faith and commitment, the road is precipitous sometimes, but there are divine hooks to hold on to while we climb, praise God.

Gilda, you'll soon have joy and satisfaction, and alert you'll still march on, as the good soldier that you are. There is nothing better in life that waking up in the morning with hope.

Sometimes we spin so much, like a carousel; life turns us into screws, trying to penetrate, to achieve and overcome, to be useful; until we learn to be of use to the world.

January 29, 2008.

(Intuition from my sister Helena's spirit.)

Peace and love sister dearest; everything is what it is; assignments must be done, corrected and finished, and turned over to the teacher.

You still need a little more concentration and dedication to these tasks, in order to leave, pleased and happy. You'll see us; yes you'll see us at any moment; I don't know when. There will be beautiful sessions amongst us, and you will do another book.

(This book; the first was in two languages, and remains the first book to the spirits.)

We have a lovely book: *(Memorias)* inspiring! God is wise; He will give us the means, I'm sure.

January 30, 2008.

(Intuition from my beloved Albert's spirit.)

God is our Savior, our light and our shelter in the long, cold nights. Malena, just like this candle that shines, is God's love; it is a source of love; we wish the world to know that they have an inexhaustible glow that warms them and guides them.

Have no fears or uncertainty; we feel covered, protected, and we will be rescued if necessary. God gives us all that, because of his infinite love, but we must appreciate it, discern, refine and respond with thoughts and actions in our daily life; thus thanking him. Health for all; the burden is lighter with health.

We all have to carry tools to open the furrows in the ground; planting is not easy; we scratch our hands, but finally see the fruit; the abundant harvest dazzles, and our happiness is immensely great.

Thus your life dearest, my Malena, with injuries and scratches in your spirit hands, but the abundant harvest makes you vibrate with satisfaction, and joy; as a soul that's pleased.

Do not think of yesterday nor tomorrow, today is enough; make today a good day with your hopes, love, peace, faith, and dreams; there are so many that don't even have one of these ingredients, they are the poor, the poorest of life. Today takes you to tomorrow; it is the continuity of the noble spirit, always breaking ground.

An Individual, who complies while maintaining an orderly line with love, and service, to others, can laugh.

February 1, 2008.

(Intuition from my sister Helena's spirit)

Peace and love sister dearest; woe the abusers; poor spirits that remain in the darkness and do not seek the light; God illuminate them, for they must pay sooner or later. Gilda, continue with a beam of light in your forehead, so that everyone can see your kindness and your love.

Loving sister don't worry about a thing; the good always wins over evil, the truth is always revealed, and faith is like money in the bank; because you can always get some, when needing resources in difficult times. Sister, we love you; many entities are your partners; remember that, and the book will be published in God's name. *(Memorias.)* Finish it.

(Intuition from my mother Monserrate.)

Daughter, you're tired, but with very little to go; you'll have relief. We, like you, are anxious, because every day is like a chapter from a novel; sometimes very badly written. Let's see what tomorrow's chapter brings; understand that we are co-creators of the script; our thoughts help to write better lines. Communication with your children is necessary; they are like sheep looking for solutions. Thank God that you can assist them with good advice; we are their invisible family and accompany them.

February 3, 2008.

(Intuition from my sister Helena's spirit.)

Peace and love sister dearest; many thanks to God's messengers. It is blissful not to have pain, to walk and fly, if so desired; someday you will know that spirit life is buoyant, weightless, lovely.

There isn't much time separating us; days go by quickly, your time doesn't exist here. We'll celebrate your homecoming.

Monserrate really, really enjoyed her incarnation in New Orleans as Isabella Karran; she loved it *(Story included in Memorias.)* She is also happy now: *"Happy Spirit"* she is now called. Bless you Gilda, for your altruism, dedication and pure love.

February 6, 2008.

(Intuition from my sister Helena's spirit.)

God blesses, and carries us all, in his arms; forgiving us, loving us, but we all have to put things in order, it's like when preparing to move to a new home; organizing, allows us to think and carry out plans carefully.

We are your invisible loving family and are always present; we see your sorrows, feel your love, and your moments of sadness and joy; that is true love. Gilda, don't worry, tomorrow is another day; we will do automatic writing together.

(Intuition from my mother Monserrate's spirit.)

Good daughter, selfless mother; we are so alike; it's impressive how similar we are. God bless my grandchildren, son, and Karym's baby girl, Vienna Skye. Those boys need you; you're representing me. Gilda, thank them for loving me so much. We know that our messages with words of encouragement always help; they are reassured because of their great faith; bless you all.

(Intuition from my beloved Albert's spirit.)

Beloved Malena, you have progressed a great deal, and you still seek more, we know it.

Soon you will have new stories for future books; the good news is that you make plans, like Helena says: organizing helps you. Many avenues await; I see a lovely and broad picture, with joy; love you all, Malena, thank you for your love.

(Automatic writing from unknown spirit.)

Yes, come, over here, I'll wait; our work is just beginning. Spirit life is a wonderful thing; your life is very boring in comparison.

We have a lot to see and to do; it is a wide, wide and majestic horizon. Sun, Moon and Stars; Universe, Firmament; our vision expands, it is much wider, enormously wide; it goes far, very far, and so are our hopes, and our love.

Compliance with God's law is our goal; all together, on behalf of the same front, in pursuit of the same ending or the same beginning. This piece of work is sensational.

February 7, 2008.

(Intuition from my sister Helena's spirit.)

Enlightenment, peace and love; all together we are marching with love, towards God; some quickly, others slower, but all united. A great light illuminates, guiding us, warming, and calming us. Together we will arrive, together we will comply, God loves and answers us Gilda, when we put all our efforts into projects of love for the world, He cares, never ceases to give us advice, inspiring us through his messengers; helping us with the cargo. They are big brothers hurrying to rescue us; you just have to have patience in order to see the results; waiting calmly, with hope; knowing that God's will is accomplished.

Something miraculous was achieved amongst all, with communications; feelings, words, emotions, wonderful passages of genuine affection; all that is in the book; making the readers think and reflect; a beautiful creation among many; wrapped in love.

We, the spirits, lived a very beautiful experience with Monserrate; she's glad knowing that she served, that she was a marvelous conductor for our voices and feelings. Those are special assignments; very few have such joy. We are right on time, with a slow but sure step; calmly going forward with this wonderful task; blessings to you, the boys, and Nel.

February 15, 2008.

(Intuition from my sister Helena's spirit. Lake.)

Peace, love, sister dearest; God blesses you, enlightens, loves us, protects and encourages us, we work on His behalf. All that love is immersed in those pages; a testament of brotherhood and love; no matter the borders; we are all one, praying for peace.

You just have to love, work and wait; it is hope and faith; sister; almost there, almost there. Calmly, don't worry; God has a small well-made package for you, it's a prize, a new sample of His love; lacking nothing. Preserve your harmony using cleverness, be patient; what you're doing is good.

You had lovely memories here by the lake; with your kind mother and all of us; memories are forever. There's peace; the birds sing the ducklings waddle. I'm leaving you a good fragment of my spirit life.
(Intuition from my beloved Albert's spirit.)

Praise God, dearest Gilda; I see you laughing; happy moments of great satisfaction.

You've learned a great deal with this book. *(First book.)* It was a major project which was in your life; you had agreed to do it while you were in spirit, Helena and you agreed; with the will and the love of God, and the assistance of our spiritual family, it has become a reality; thank you Father, and brothers.

March 22, 2008.

(Intuition from my sister Helena's spirit.)

Peace and love sister dear; what has happened is lovely Gilda, you've changed, you've improved. It has been a rough road, full of thorns and scratches; you've been injured, but the scars are dissipating.

It is love, will, and faith in operation; you have not forgotten: *"To yearn for; is power."* Immense joy and satisfaction, for us to see that we have served you; that our words and prayers, are not lost, and you, share them with your boys and your brother.
(Intuition from my mother Monserrate's spirit.)

Gilda, beloved daughter; you have adjusted well; nobody takes away your harmony; I also did that, It's the magic formula to be happy. The birds are your companions, your divine choir; they inject you with energy as they sing; it is a great serenade between the Universe and earth sounds.

I helped to fulfill some of your goals; to polish your skills and your talent, so I'm happy; we worked and we grew together; those are pleasant memories.

I also remember my fears; thanks for sheltering me, you always looked after me; I was like a scared child. Now you protect and care for the loose papers with my writings; it's a beautiful gift that you have given me, I did not expect so much, thank you. The work that you are finishing is a privilege;

God gives such a task to very few; continue developing your flowery delicacy to share with the world in a communication vast, and eternal; it is light for the blind with sight, but no vision.

March 23, 2008.

(Intuition from my sister Helena's spirit.)

Peace and love sister dearest; Happy Easter Sunday; dear Jesus, thank you for your love and your peace. The message of resurrection is very powerful, it confirms eternal life; resurrection is God's love and forgiveness, giving us another chance; that forgiveness allows us to start all over. Glory to God!

Gilda, remember everything moves, everything flows, nothing is stationary; it's all about the current being positive; we activate the positive energy with love and our thoughts; shaping our environment, our physical scene, with our thoughts, so it is.

I bring as a gift; a few bunnies from the Universe for your granddaughter "*Vienna Skye*"; they jump, do cartwheels and say "*I love you, I love you.*"

(Intuition from my beloved Albert's spirit.)

Beloved Malena, our souls are bonded, our souls communicate; you conceive my thoughts well. It is wonderful and rare, in a world so wide, a blessing; I am grateful to God. You're doing a great art piece, only a few touches left; Monserrate tells me to congratulate you; we all do; everyone.

May God continue to illuminate you beloved, I am glad that you read the lyrics of the tango *"Malena"* It's an old tango, based on a play in which you participated; something from our past. We have been together several times; Albert was Alejandro.

The story is like this; first I was Elpidio, later Albert, but I also lived in Spain; loving you since then; they are exquisite stories of eternal love. We have lived, loved and suffered a great deal, but the road is wider and cleaner now; that is why God gives us this happiness. I have much to tell you; soon you will hear us; there will be verbal communications, something so lovely, so beautiful; we're all branches that love each other. I'm grateful; I never tire of thanking God for the communications.

(Intuition from my mother Monserrate's spirit.)

Beloved daughter; we, the three sisters, are very happy; we make our rounds in your world and the Universe; we traveled with our parents, talking to them; it is something magnificent. I'm eager to speak *"Face"* to *"Face"* with you; in some form it will be.

March 27, 2008.

(Intuition from my sister Helena's spirit.)

Peace, love, sister dearest; thank God we have spiritual and physical health to achieve our goals, an effort is always needed, sometimes superhuman, for everything, because of the many obstacles; but with faith, determination and devotion, it gets easier and we see results sooner or later.

Extraordinary things happen when you combine these elements with Divine Grace and the assistance of the spiritual brothers; creating a very powerful magnetic force. Nothing is impossible for God and His messengers.

Gilda, you are more receptive, it's the peace in your soul; take care, guard it; difficult to acquire. Yes, Albert was Alexander; I like how you get the hints, just like you did, in the past.

The story is very beautiful; yes, he was looking for you in Puerto Rico; there was a little confusion of dates and he did not find you, but here you have him; God is Good, Generous and Merciful; you'll know more.
(Intuition from my beloved Albert's spirit.)

Beloved Malena, if you only knew what awaits you, it is a brilliant path of lights; a path that we have built together with our faith and love of God. It is a blue road, because the pure light looks blue.

Each one has been a laborer, lifting the stones, putting them in place. Completed the route, we will all undertake the journey; bringing our messages to the world. I repeat that discipline is so important in any world, discipline is harmony and that harmony brings peace, allowing love to flourish with intensity.

The body's density makes us clumsy, feeling numb; that is why we must be more spiritual on earth, more spirit; that is the truth, spiritual life is exquisite. Albert loves Malena; I'm always nearby, hugging you with my wings.

April 10, 2008.

(Intuition from my sister Helena's spirit.)

Peace, dearest sister, love and light to be able to continue contributing to the spiritual liberation of our brothers on earth. With your devotion, little by little you've woven a large multicolored, thick, but light, blanket, to cover many from the cold; a fabric that will last, and will be appreciated. Mysticism is sought, and it attracts. Thank you Father for the means to achieve all this; Gilda you receive our messages like email.

(Intuition from my mother Monserrate's spirit.)

I'm happy daughter to see so much beauty and to do charitable work. Learning from nature; everything catches my attention, and I never tire of looking at so many wonders. I can't explain it, but over here, it's like life over there, but without pains or sorrows, and with a sense of relief, of love and unique peace.

We talk, we laugh, and we share, but we also have tasks that we gladly do; we take breaks to see our love ones, we pray for you; wanting to protect you, and we are aware of everything.

Our love is great, you have no idea. God shows us His love and power all the time, you just have to fix your eyes and be thankful. I visit you, and am glad to see the good things that are coming your way; we hug you all, on a daily basis; I love you.

May 2, 2008.

(Intuition from my sister Helena's spirit.)

Peace and love sister dearest, I'm glad to see you so dedicated to prayer; you have progressed much. Prayer is a very strong tonic, giving vigor and, fortitude; allowing you to fly with your thoughts. Never doubt, blessings are there at your disposal; whatever our Father has, is there to take, you just have to make an effort and take it; life becomes simpler, things are easier when you extend your hand to God, so that He may guide you.

June 10, 2008.

(With my sons in NYC.)

(Intuition from my sister Helena's spirit.)

Peace, love, sister dearest; how many times did your mother pray for you? Mothers always care for their young, great love binds them; the most beautiful emotion on earth. Bless all good mothers.

Things will improve; cycles of satisfaction are ahead; our book will give much joy; arriving as light; illuminating, leaving traces in the souls of many. God and brothers' thank you.

(Intuition from my mother Monserrate's spirit.)

Dearest daughter, I'm closer now, and have the lightness that I always desired; feeling stronger, ready; it is a unique feeling. My life as a spirit is lovely, lovely, you cannot imagine. Gilda you will be very happy here; what you have not found there, will be waiting for you here, the love of your life; Albert, bless him. When you return it will be a great day!

I'm happy seeing you and the boys together, it's a beautiful dream of love and tenderness; they are my life, even in spirit.

(Intuition from my beloved Albert's spirit.)

My beloved Malena, you have learned that life is not so difficult when you row with the current, thus you are peaceful; acclimating to the changes and difficulties; they don't surprise you; knowing how to deal with them, that is a blessing.

You are mentally secluded from the world; that also helps to concentrate on your work; those are wise technics; later on you will have time to share and enjoy; I know that you don't miss it. The book is being polished; we embrace and are grateful to God and the many entities that have worked with you on the manuscript; the big day is approaching; love you.

June 27, 2008.

(Intuition from my beloved Albert's spirit.)

Beloved Malena, light of my life; someday I will tell you more about our story. Books and booklets are on the way, just a bit more to go.

Making good use of your time; your commitment is impressive; behaving as a spirit in search of light, for the sake of progress.

The world wants to learn; there's a disparity of paths, eventually adjusting. You'll bring light and joy to many souls; offering our books to alleviate them, in God's name. That's why we ask for light to see the whole picture, not bits and pieces.

We are brave soldiers in a major battle between goodness and ignorance; with strong armor, solid, impenetrable; it's our love, our faith and the help of God and the enlightened entities. Stones and shells pass by closely, without touching us. Every day we can learn and climb, approaching God with peace and confidence in our strength, and His protection.

Malena there is a lush and flowery path for you, and soon you'll get there; it's part of the results of your great effort. Little by little, push the cart full of your gifts to the world; the cart is heavy, but there are many who want to give you a hand, relieving you, taking it to our brothers who expect good news. Those are things of the soul; profound things will come to you.

Your life has been intense, full of experiences; always enriching your spirit; and it's reflected in your work. Think that you're a baker and you are making a cake, a delicious cake; there will be many pieces to share; it will be appetizing to many; asking for more.

Don't be afraid; follow what your conscience tells you, because there are multiple ways in which God speaks to us; guiding and leadings us; you just have to give way to His inspiration; just listen calmly. God cares for you; your friends in spirit carry you. We need your organism *(Body)* in top condition, and it will be. I love you, Malena, I love all of you.

August 4, 2008.

(Intuition from my sister Helena's spirit.)

Peace and love sister dearest. How beautiful it is to feel peace, and to have a goal in life. With peace you're a millionaire, the treasure is hidden in your soul. Always be receptive to God's love, and constructive ideas to benefit humanity; everything is wonderful in God's garden.

(Intuition from my mother Monserrate's spirit.)

Daughter dearest, go on, you'll have the skills to complete the task; thank you for loving us so very much, we love you the same way. You feel us when we embrace you; perception will increase with more serenity. God's messengers inspire and help you; they are wise and patient; they come and go like a breath, like lightning.

Blessings to everyone; I'm content recalling your radio programs; feeling gratitude for sharing those moments with you, daughter; I do feel joyful.

These are spectacular moments for many over here; they are present, and have come to greet, and thank you, for the past interviews; for your sincere interest in presenting their talents to the world. They say: *"Thank you"* all in chorus: *"Thank you Gilda."* Praise God! Daughter, in the past you had superb inspiration and you still do; calmly you will achieve your goals.

(Intuition from my beloved Albert's spirit.)

My beloved Malena, answers to your questions you will have; you will know more about our spiritual development; surprising, fascinating, and beautiful; you know that we searched; found each other, and we will always love each other.

August 16, 2008.

(Intuition from my sister's Helena's spirit.)

Peace, love, sister dearest; every day can be a pretty adventure when there is faith, hope, and love. We make of our lives what we desire; definitely our thoughts influence events.

Gilda, now you're lighter, more spiritual, this is a blessing; the book has transformed you, reviewing, copying the conversations with the spirits so often, has touched your soul.

The messages must get out, clear and precise. Remember what I told you about our previous life; our motto was, *"Promptness and Dedication."* (*Tutors and translators, in "Five Points" N.Y.C. Circa 1840; more in my first book.*)

You will take our messages of love, peace and eternal life to many places; a large number of people will accept you; they will believe, and follow advice. A sublime, beautiful, exclusive mission; thank God.

(Intuition from my mother Monserrate's spirit.)

Daughter, I often think of our life together; thank you for sharing so many beautiful moments with me. I feel enormous satisfaction and joy, seeing the results of the messages that came through me, with God's permission; the guides, our spiritual family and protective spirits assistance.

(Intuition from my beloved Albert's spirit.)

Talent, faith, awareness of self, a commitment to God; those are very powerful and blessed elements in this journey; a cooperation between two worlds; we cannot ask for more, but thank God.

August 24, 2008.

(Intuition from my sister Helena's spirit.)

Peace, love sister dearest, faith is the bright star guiding us, allowing us to move ahead on a dark night. You have a star Gilda; it is your ardent desire to share; to give to the world our messages of love and faith, and the help you receive, given by God; that serves as a consolation; because you are not alone, there are brothers loving you, talking to you in the ear and whispering ideas.

You were stuck. *(Measurements required by the printer.)* You calculated, over and over, but weren't getting results, but you searched and asked for help, and it was resolved; the messengers came to assist you; God's gifts. He knows exactly what you need, our gratitude to His messengers;

Everything is harmonious in the Universe; when there is harmony in our lives, everything is smoother, it flows, glides; so it will be with our book; quickly it will take flight, because it contains love and peace; it is an invitation to hope, and believe in God.

January 11, 2009.

(Intuition from my sister Helena's spirit.)

Peace and love sister dearest; I ask for more light; may all the lights be lit to be able to see well.

Our souls rejoice because we know that we are working properly. Our consciences are at peace, and we're happy; that is the greatest happiness, the peace of knowing that we are unsoiled. We must seek the good avenues, broad roads and leafy sidewalks, with sun and cool breezes.

You and Monserrate received much love and responded; with lifetimes full of sacrifices and pure feelings, with great faith. Understand that the spirits are duty-bound; we can't make decisions for mortals, it's not our mission, we can only encourage, so that humans know that God loves them; that an army of benevolent spirits are present; praying and working for the good of all.

February 11, 2009.

(Intuition from my sister Helena's spirit.)

Everything, everything, is always moving there is nothing static or affixed; motion and harmony are essential in the Universe; our lives, and evolution.

We are extremely happy with your peace and your discipline; you've grown little sister, but you must still learn some more. We urge you to continue climbing the boulders which sometimes look very high, but as we approach them they seem smaller and we can climb them.

Life is like a ladder, step by step; it seems that we're going to fall, but we don't, we go on; holding on to our faith, our love of God, and then taking another step up. We dare not look back or down, for fear of falling, but even then, looking away we are not falling, because we are all firmly fastened to God with calmness and persistence. God bless everyone, especially the little children, who are so helpless. Peace on earth.

(Intuition from my beloved Albert's spirit.)

There are so many things to tell you, beloved Malena. Our evolutions are parallel; meaning that we are living experiences together.

Each in their own dimension; but growth is mutual; it's somewhat complex, but at the same time simple; nothing remains immobile, everything moves, nothing is stagnant.

Love is the driving force, faith generates; always creating the energy needed, and maintaining upward movements. Together we are all achieving; you help us and vice versa.

(Intuition from my mother Monserrate's spirit.)

Daughter dear, I am always close by; you are all my beautiful and fragrant buds; it's a lovely garden that we have, and we are all gardeners.

Let the whole world see that there is a Supreme Intelligence, loving and listening to them. When our Creator places His hand; all our affairs ease up, as constant proof of His love and intervention.

February 15, 2009.

(Intuition from my sister Helena's spirit.)

Peace, love, sister dearest; every time you read the messages: *(From Memorias.)* it will arouse your emotions, because it was with divine assistance that you were able to accomplish it. We still have much more to tell you; it will come, and it will surprise you greatly. Monserrate is very content; and with good reason; she transmitted; elaborated the messages, working hard and motivating all of you with her good seeds; giving magnificent fruits.

(Intuition from my mother Monserrate's spirit.)

I don't know how many times to tell you how happy I am about the book! We know God sent you His assistants, but I'm amazed how you recapped their instructions; it turned out lovely, thank God.

May 17, 2009.

(Intuition from unknown spirit.)

In the name of Almighty God; enlightenment yes, ask for light, always asking for illumination, to see a brighter road, and to love all. We foresee joy in your souls and lives.

Enlightened spirits, thank you; may God support you all. Our Creator is kind-hearted, wise, all-loving; forgiving many offenses, pettiness and nonsense; *(Stopped channeling.)* He knows well what is at the bottom of our hearts. We are happy with your endeavors; little by little, you will feel more strength, health, wellbeing, and the desire to fulfill this task.

December 5, 2009.

(Translating, "Memorias" book to English.)

(Intuition from my sister Helena's spirit)

Peace, love, sister dearest; congratulating you on your well received inspirations. We are willing to assist with God's permission; you have been more receptive lately and that makes us happy because you are developing. More surprises will come, very, very, pleasant ones.

April 12, 2010.

(Intuition from my sister Helena' spirit)

Peace and love sister dearest; it has been long since we last spoke face to face; but we are always present, even at a distance, our souls are joined by love and affinity. We have blessed commitments and are determined to fulfill them. God's fresh rain will wipe the trail clean, and we'll be able to look at the sky in all its majesty, bringing us Universal fresh winds; calming our spirits.

Nothing moves without the will of God. He is Generous; listening to our prayers. We're witnesses of His Benevolence and love; always responding, although in His own way, knowing what is best for us; all requests have an answer.

April 17, 2010.

(Intuition from my sister Helena's spirit.)

Peace, love sister dearest; illumination for all; enlightenment and more light, there is never enough light; now and forever.

We are many; all linked by boundless love, keeping an eye on you; we monitor and listen to your requests. Everything is moving along according to a spiritual improvement project; learning, progressing; every day taking one step further, one more lesson. We all have to be good students to graduate.

April 20, 2010.

(Intuition from my sister Helena's spirit.)

Peace and love sister dearest; I bring good vibrations from the Universe; immense, pure, sincere love; not gray, sad or painful, but eternal, and brilliant as the Sun. We wish to hug you all; you're our protégés; not wanting anything negative to hurt you, on the contrary; may there be gayety, joy, health, and songs in your lives.

It's blissful to see the results of our sowing; seeing the books in your hands. *(Published books in English*

& Spanish.) Thanks to the enlightened entities contributing to these works, but there will be others. There's still time to work, leaving more seeds on earth, from the noble spirits. I encourage you brothers; wide doors will open.

April 23, 2010.

(Intuition from my sister Helena's spirit.)

Peace and love sister dear; review your life and see how much God has helped you. Your guardian angel has been very busy, and we are grateful.

We all want our brothers to open their eyes; to know God is Fair and Generous, that life continuous; He loves us and shows it daily. We're bound by love and respect, supporting each other; as usual, God forgiving and cuddling us.

Winds come in through the window all the time, some refresh, others are warm, but we must keep the window open, watching out for bad currents; everything is like that; even with the spirits.

Our souls just like boats; are always sailing, looking for a sure port to refurbish. There is a large lighthouse guiding us, it's our Creator; let us follow His light, it always leads to a safe harbor.

We must understand that human beings are capricious, and that's why we must practice piety, cultivating patience. Sooner or later they must learn; the blows teach us. Nothing, nothing, is lost in our path, we collect in two baskets, the good and the less good. We must empty the negative, cleaning up our baskets.

Gilda; soon we will begin to share valuable information for another book; yes, for another

book. *(This book)* Changes will occur, adjustments made, but with patience you will do it in harmony.

April 26, 2010.

(Intuition from unknown spirit.)

It's fascinating to think about all that we can be! We can be happy, successful and healthy; all that is obtainable, we just have to get on the right track and follow through; thoughts and actions in unison.

Bless the ones that realize their potential and go for it; working tirelessly; enduring, staying on path. Do we know which way to go, or where to turn? No! But we perceive it, we feel it; the enlightened spirits put us on automatic pilot, guiding us. How wonderful and beautiful it all feels, and is!

Do not stray from your goal, do not desist, or drop your dreams, they are there for you to grasp and to hold. Today may be raining and stormy, tomorrow the sun will shine again; even brighter than before. Warmth will overcome the chilly air.

April 27, 2010.

(Intuition from my sister Helena's spirit.)

Peace and love sister dearest; as always, when it's possible, we approach you; any time it's good to feel God and his messengers.

Well done your efforts to promote the books, it is important; sooner or later it will bear fruit. *(Working on website.)* Your life is beautiful, productive, and the (5) books are realities, not fantasies; soon the trips will come.

There are no disappointments or disillusions; you've seen the results of faith; the obstacles were demolished, doors opened, answers arrived. That's

God's work and each person with their faith and purpose working together, it's no coincidence.

Illumination, peace, love, are the ingredients for this great mix; or *"Shake"* that you enjoy so much; we are inviting you to drink with us.

May 1, 2010.

(Intuition from unknown spirit.)

You say: what's there for me? You ask yourself constantly. It's logical and normal to wonder; and yet nobody knows what tomorrow will bring; you are making your tomorrow, today; yes, you are molding, sketching, and embellishing your tomorrow in your fashion, it is hard to believe, but it is quite true.

Watch your thoughts, your dreams, your words and actions; because they are your paintbrushes and sculpturing tools; helping you create that unknown tomorrow. It is not difficult; it's challenging and easy, I would say; maintain your harmony and peace.

Focus on your desires, hopes and goals. Are those wishes wise? Are they grounded, practical, positive, well balanced; without extremes? You are the artist that can answer all that. Only you can give the right touches and tones to your canvas or to the molding clay of life.

May your palette be pretty, colorful and plentiful so as not to use murky colors, or be without paint, in the midst of your inspiration. Find the right hues, and tones, and you surely, will create a beautiful picture.

May 2, 2010.

(Intuition from my sister Helena's spirit.)

Peace, love, sister dearest; we're ready and willing to speak on a daily basis; yes, you started automatic writing, but lost the pace; things happen that get in the way or divert us. God is Generous and Wise; forgiving us every moment, instantaneously; so we can begin again.

You ask: what's ahead for me? You ask a sound question; it deserves an answer; think, count the many things on your plate to do now, and in the future. The list is long, and you ask; where do I start? It's also a good question.

Start at the beginning. What comes first? You know well! What's in your heart? Love comes first; the love of God, of family, of life, of neighbor, and love of work; all that is on the list.

Find out what your second move is. How? By thinking, understanding and analyzing your needs; only you know them. Speak to God about them; have an intimate chat with God. He will assign his messengers to your special needs and pleas; it works, believe me it works; try it.

May 10, 2010.

(Intuition from unknown spirit. Lake.)

You see, you can write; try, try, and try, things will happen unexpectedly; we must prepare, and sometimes, prevent; be smart. How can anyone doubt God's righteousness; He's always present in everything; look at the leaves moving, they think that they're dancing and singing; the Universe is smiling, the entire Universe thanks God for His kindness.

Yesterday was good; *(My eldest son surprised me with his visit, and we enjoyed "Mother's Day")*

It was God's gift; stay tranquil, the harvest will come; no more uncertainties.

May 23, 2010.
(Intuition from my sister Helena's spirit.)

There are always labyrinths in that world; it is part of the compromise, and evolution, but we learn to unknot the strings and to put them in order; with great hope and abundant faith; those are major forces driving the positive developments.

All this exercise *(Complications)* has served for abundant progress; it's not negative, it has been positive; there's more appreciation of everything; now developing the art of living and not existing.

Everyone learns their way, and at their speed; but we all learn sooner or later, that is why we are here, and we don't want to repeat lessons. Praise God and thanks to our enlightened brothers.

June 8, 2010.
(Intuition from unknown spirit.)

We are Universal spiritual entities; and by choice or divine mandate, have been sent to this earthly world in order to experience human life, to learn, and to grow in love. Eventually enlightened, we will reach our goal; Universal Consciousness, which is God. We are truly much bigger than what you call life! We hope that these messages will inspire many humans to recognize their immortality.

June 22, 2010
(Intuition from unknown spirit.)

Climb the highest mountain joyfully, with a song in your heart, sing to the trees, to the birds, and to the sky. Share your inspiration and your happiness, it's all fine. Wonderment you will feel, as you stride; and weightlessness will carry you far. All this occurs when your mind is not tied down to the mundane; buoyant you will feel; light as a feather, singing with the wind; not a cloud in the sky.

God only knows where you will land in your reverie; but your heart and your soul are lively, joyful and serene.

There is no magic, no secret formula to all this; just love, love, and love, leading you on; as you comply in little, and in big ways, in this your present earthly condition, and you move on.

June 24, 2010.

(Intuition from my sister Helena's spirit.)

Peace, love, sister dearest; light in your path so as not to stumble; you're tired of dragging yourself around; wanting to walk upright, firm, straight up; knowing where you're going. Keep walking, because the grand trip is coming. You'll have wings, sister; wings.

With light and joy the shadows dissipate, and we see the sunshine at a distance. The road is clear; no thorns, there are no stones and there is no danger of tripping. Each day moving one step forward, never backward, or remaining motionless; there's no other option, but to go forward in God's path.

August 27, 2010.

(Intuition from unknown spirit. Lake)

Peace and love, Gilda Mirós; we are many friends, loves from yesteryear; in quest of peace; evolving, studying, loving, assisting; it is all linked. Gilda, there are no stones in your path, just pebbles that you can avoid. Better days are coming sister, you can believe it; days of peace, harmony, laughter and joy, Yes, yes, the spirits bring you space flowers as a gift to you; they are lovely.

What a beautiful landscape; come to this lake more often, it helps you very much. Everyone is in a hurry and you are calm, looking at God, don't worry about the time, it does not exist; rejoice.

Your mother is by your side with Helena and Albert; they observe and kiss you.

September 4, 2010.

(Intuition from unknown spirit.)

Peace opens the door for inspiration or intuition. If it's lost at times, it can be recovered, when there is faith and a willingness to look for it.

We all have ups and downs; its evolution, life and circumstances; outside influences affect us, for example: wayward entities nearby, approach us or maybe negative thoughts fired by them, from long distance; in short, a constant bombardment. We are recipients of all this, according to our sensibilities; therefore learn to discern and catalog thoughts, in order to live in peace, it's almost an art, or a studied discipline; and we assume that over the years, we improve our understanding and our behavior, related to all this matter.

Health is affected by all this surrounding invisible commotion; and physical resistance is weakened, so you must create a wall of spiritual, mental and emotional defenses; a whole army of self-defense.

Becoming familiar with what's happening, your spiritual forces, discipline, faith and hope, keep you well harmonized; that is ideal, but sometimes, with the aging process, the defenses weaken; strength is neglected, getting slower, discouraged; exposed to all the ills and diseases of society. Unfortunately this option is very common.

We must disclose; *"Spread the word"* that's all in life; everything is in our thoughts and in our hands and not only in God's hands.

He gives us free will, and the tools; allowing his messengers to inspire us and help us, but the work is ours.

Make your lives a song of love and gratitude to God, with your thoughts and actions. The echo of the heavenly singing will calm and elevate you, guiding you to new and better areas. All that depends on the ideas and the peaceful states of mind in which we find ourselves, and finally understanding that there is immense spiritual abundance and prosperity within our reach; in other words, happiness and comfort, do not cost anything, only some courage, and the sacrifice to calm ourselves; plus a sincere desire to receive it.

Humans are slow learners; wanting things easy; served on a silver platter, and even then, they don't see or digest them; beautiful and positive elements bypass them, flying over their heads.

October 1, 2010.

(Intuition from unknown spirit. Lake)

I have come to bring you peace sister; like this lake, keep your soul in harmony, not in agony; there is peace here; it's a source of inspiration; nature's sounds are the chants of God's love.

There is nothing to fear or to search for; things that suit you will come; yes, thoughts and faith are magnets that attract events, affecting our daily lives. Search in your soul for the stillness, it is there in your noble feelings. You've been able to assist, to help your children, especially the small, man/child; he thanks you very much.

Your sister Helena is here; also Monserrate and Albert. I'm one more brother, loving; sustaining you.

February 2, 2011.

(Intuition from my sister Helena's spirit.)

Peace and love sister dearest; open your eyes, wonderful things are happening, a result of active faith, just as you read in the many spirit books, so it is; we must keep believing, loving, working steadily.

In your gray world, there are always ordeals, but the sun shines and warms us; the sun is God. He embraces us with nature, kisses us with the breeze, and gives us rest at night; always Wise. We must believe no matter what! Believe in God and in the assistance of the spirits.

Let's help with our messages; they will learn. Promote your books; they'll move; the issue is to spread the seeds.

April 6, 2011.

(Intuition from unknown spirit.)

Things are moving quickly, soon you'll see it; these are not words, they are realities. Commitments you'll have; travel and interviews will materialize. Your freedom will come in part, because it is never total in your world. Beautiful things occur as a result of faith, self-sacrifice, and perseverance.

April 8, 2011.

(Intuition from unknown son's spirit.)

Mother of mine, you do not know me, but I know you. We were mother and son, more than a century ago, in another very distant and warm land. Those days were beautiful, cheerful, with love, peace, and joy. It was a family atmosphere; lovely, lovely.

My name does not matter for now; you will know it; I promise. Love traces remain forever; caring and caresses are impregnated in the spirit eternally.

Let me tell you a beautiful story; you like stories; you're an actress. We shared with another that came with you now; we were family; caring and searching for each other, from lifetime to lifetime. That's all for now; we will continue the story. I love you, blessings.

April 9, 2011.

(Intuition from unknown son's spirit.)

Let's continue with the story so longed by you. First, I'll tell you that I have never seen so much glory as the one, for the spirit. Mother, your world is so grey and sad. Here everything shines and vibrates! It is really what they call heavenly. I would like to share that feeling and experience with you; transmit it to you, so that you may vibrate equally with God's love.

Perceiving so much bitterness saddens you, and your spiritual defenses are weakened. No, not that; you have the antidote, faith, love, charity and hope. I love you, blessings.

April 12, 2011.

(Intuition from the spirit of unknown son.)

Yes mother, your thoughts are correct. We lived together when you were *"Xavrina."* My uncle was then *"Druahl",* your brother Nel, now. *(In first book there is data about a past incarnation in Turkey, with my current brother Nel. A musical family; dancing with two brothers; a sad, but lovely story.)*

I too joined the group of dancers; dancing since childhood, loving music and dancing; I was attractive and strong, agile like you; dancing kept us in optimal conditions. Those were days of artistic triumph. We had success and fame in our local environment; not any further, because they were difficult times and the distances were extensive. We will continue the story. I love you mother.

April 13, 2011.

(Intuition from unknown son's spirit.)

Peace, love, dear mother; there is so much love and happiness amongst all.

It's painful to see so many humans crawling with the chains of the body; they are prisoners of their old habits. God gives us freedom of action; it is a very special gift, the freedom to think, to do; when we are bound by circumstances we rebel, it's natural. Those are your tantrums; *"Mood Swings"*

We must understand what afflicts us, and control it, because it hinders our development; don't let it stop your upward march. That's what's wrong with you; wanting to be free! But you are; yesterday, the backup needed arrived; thus freeing your actions.

Thank you Father, enlightened spirits, because it has been a huge task for all; we have all assisted carrying a large rock. Now your sons can give you the necessary push to continue working.

God is Wise, Generous and Merciful; loving us. The spirits provide purpose, energy and prayers to our Creator, assisting our incarnated brothers. The task is just beginning; take firm, positive steps. Many blessings are waiting for you. I love you mother.

April 14, 2011.

(Intuition from unknown son's spirit.)

Peace, peace mother. In what way can I tell you the truth? Nothing is easy in that life, you know it well; stumbling, falling, we get up and continue; so it is! There is no more to say; that's why we can't stay behind, no; there are goals; commitments to fulfill.

We develop spiritual vitality as we deal with the facts; recuperate, pick ourselves up and continue; that's all; until the desired day arrives.

There are, and there will be; wide, spacious and clean paths, with roses kissing our hands. It's all an up and down of emotions, but creating in us, clarity of thought, determination and purpose; that is the commitment. I love you mother.

April 15, 2011.

(Intuition from unknown son's spirit.)

Peace, illumination, love, progress, all essential to evolve, to be happy. There are billions of people without the compass of faith. It is blissful to have faith! Expecting good, positive things; knowing that abundance will come, if not material, spiritual; that's to have faith.

A pardon for those ignorant, indifferent humans, they will learn in time; although there is so much time lost. They don't do, or undo, they are just there. In life we must work, that's why we're here; it is a commitment with God and with ourselves; showing gratitude with actions; which our achievements are.

It is never too late to learn, to improve; it is a matter of willingness to do so. Benevolent Creator, thank Thee, for always giving us another opportunity.

Mother, there will be time to talk and write; love you.

April 17, 2011.

(Intuition from unknown spirit.)

Gilda, dearest; yes, it is faith that propels you. What better generator of corporeal and spiritual force is there? Every day it is stronger, and it never lacks momentum. Keep your mind, your receiver open, properly set, to receive messages and missions.

You will have many more invitations to speak about faith, love, discipline and purpose in life. You're an example, and good examples are shown, because they motivate, inspiring others. You're our ambassador; a correspondent.

Love, is the password for everything and in everything, it is the elixir of our lives; here and there. Peace and love for you, sister, mother; rejoice for the things coming; lovely, positive and wonderful events for you, your love ones, and humankind.

April 21, 2011.

(Intuition from my sister Helena's spirit)

Peace and love, dear sister, write this: you know very well, that very positive things are coming, you perceive them. Unexpected projects will appear in communications as your brother said; I can not tell you how, but it is coming; part of God's plan for disclosure; and you requested it. *(Helena requested, to be used by God, as an instrument of His love and peace; I asked for the same thing.)*

Sister, you will serve as an instrument to carry messages to the world; with abilities to use, missions to accomplish. The proposal starts small; it will grow with the success expected, and achieved. You have the best producer, director, and promoter: God.

Remain tranquil, you can't lose an iota of peace, you'll need it for your work; peace is essential for creativity; ideas will flow to you in calmness.

May 1, 2011.
(Intuition from unknown spirit.)

Peace Father, peace to the world that moans, cries, twisting. Love, progress and relief for the souls asking for help; left with nothing.

(Earthquakes, hurricanes) Angels, advanced spirits, assist them; helping them, giving them strength and energy; inspiring positive, constructive ideas; how to solve, how to improve their situations. Good ideas are gifts from God; healthy seeds can germinate and give good fruits, as you've seen.

Let's glorify our Omnipotent, Generous, God, for His abundant love; His Powerful Hand looks after us, protecting, offering gifts; a banquet full of blessings; we observe His Benevolence daily, surprising us.

I've come to bring peace and harmony to all; encouragement, and a desire to yearn, Gilda; that I want to pass on to you; although you're filed with aspirations. Working together, improving situations with love, commitment; building bridges of friendship, fraternity, with clear comprehensive communications.

That's how we grow, and we evolve; complying with our Immense, Merciful Creator; the Universe. Learn to see Him, as He really is; clear, pure; all enlightenment, perennial illumination; eternal love.

Sister, get on with your mission; doors, and also windows will open soon; you'll enter with suitcases full of books; writings, all blessed, ready to distribute.

Monserrate was an extraordinary medium; she will return to this planet with greater faculties to serve others. You and your brother, will return with her, with a respectable mission. Your sister Helena has advanced;

she is at a higher level, but she will not abandon you. She cares; loving you all, like now; assisting from that other level; thank you Father for such joy.

May 13, 2011.

(Intuition from unknown spirit.)

Love, patience, enlightenment, perseverance, and peace; also wisdom in your actions; these are all essential elements in the spirit's evolution.

Mission accomplished or breached; but with the desire to give, to love, and to share that love with our brothers; it's a spiritual ecstasy from shared love. Thank God for both; having and loving each other, forever.

To have faith is beautiful; it definitely saves us. Sister, understand this well: life and your mission are not complex, but rather simple. Praise God for His presence in your lives, through the voices of the spiritual entities. Tell the world that God loves them, yes, repeat, that God loves them; wiser words do not exist. Good ideas, interests, and divine inspiration will come. There will be opportunities to work, and you will work in the name of God.

May 17, 2011.

(Intuition from my sister Helena's spirit. Lake)

Peace and love sister, you're always the same inquisitive, naive and good little girl. God blesses you for your noble spirit, your purity and your desire to comply; *"No matter what."*

You're blessed! Stopping to look, appreciate and enjoy the face of God; which is nature's beauty. I like seeing your tranquility, regaining peace; serenely continue with your tasks; that are quite a few, and lovely like your spirit. We are all here, hugging, strengthening you with real hopes and positive facts; follow your intuition. Enlightened spirits come and go with messages, inspirations, and warnings.

You'll achieve want you want dear sister, and when your time comes, it will be triumphant, with beautiful feelings and pretty emotions of a desired reunion with family and friends, that are waiting.

June 1, 2011.

(Intuition from my sister Helena's spirit.)

Maturity of the spirit is so important in dealing with incarnation situations; many lack that attribute. Uneven roads there are many, always, but there are also beautiful, wide avenues; beautiful ideas to cultivate; works to complete, and paths to retrace in God's name.

June 17, 2011.

(Intuition from my beloved Albert's spirit.)

I brought you a sunflower Malena; that is my gift. There are simple and beautiful things in life; you just have to look, observe, appreciate and implement; stopping to recover vigor lost in the struggle for life.

Follow your inspirations, create; art is, and has always been important in your many lifetimes. Art is calming; it's the best antidote for stress; the mind focuses on the positive side; the spirit reaches a higher element, acquiring beneficial energy. Creative work encourages; giving you a pick-up, it's a tonic. Thank God you follow your ideas; the creative spirit is happy and unhappy at times, because of great sensitivity, feeling everything deeply; with moments of ecstasy and sharing them with the world.

June 18, 2011.
(*Intuition from my sister Helena's spirit.*)

Peace and love dearest sister; yes, your books are the product of faith, persistence, devotion, and the beautiful inspirations that you've received; wise, and solid messages from these loving souls, who want to enlighten the world; sharing their love and teachings.

The world is all scrambled; completely deranged with the love of money, all the materialistic; it is a contagious disease, even reaching children. Humans must control their impulses, their fickle ways; each one must do their utmost to control and correct themselves. There're so many emotions; a whirlwind of feelings; good, bad, and indifferent.

That has been your life Gilda; with more positives than negatives and no evil; ignorance, professional and personal insecurities. Tomorrow will be another beginning, more active and positive, new; thus it will be until you leave that nearsighted world.

God always has something in His inkwell for you; because you've earned it. There's plenty to do; we must go on; there will be peace, health, everything needed to work. The messages will continue arriving; they are from different entities that are collaborating. The negativity will pass; only love and God remain.

June 22, 2011.
(*Intuition from spirit, friendly musician,*)

Gilda, I'm bringing love from God and the spirits. Joyfulness! Glorious extensive laughter of spiritual rejuvenation, no tears; the sad moments or minutes of discord dissipate quickly, you must forget; only remember the joviality, the satisfaction and delight of good sense, good living; of complying with your duty.

You have communicated much good; yes, doing charity over the years with your words; continue doing it; channels will open, paths, frequencies; you will succeed again.

July 5, 2011.

(Intuition from unknown spirit.)

Let us celebrate life! Let's conquer our fears and discontent, knowing that good tidings will reach us; that we are aware of God's love and benevolence.

Yes, earth life is an enigma, with many surprises; sometimes many questions unanswered, but we definitely know that light outshines darkness.

We constantly ask: what will be? Who knows? God knows; the possibilities are many; mostly up to us. He's the greatest of the great! Loving us all, no matter what. Let's thank him for the gifts that pick us up; elevating our spirits above our miseries. All is not lost; never, never, there is always a way; we always find a path.

Enlightened is my name; illuminated I am. Let me enlighten you too, so that you may follow the straight path, the path of light, of illumination.

You're compassionate; that's why you have great patience; lovely and good for the soul. Benevolence and patience are the way to progress; and intentions are as important as actions. Don't doubt it; Universal vigor is within you. Nothing ends; it's recycled matter.

July 9, 2011.

(Intuition from unknown spirit.)

Attraction between spirits and humans greatly influence evolution; because thoughts are magnets that attract the positive or the negative. Thoughts are frequency, and the stronger the minds of the sender, or the recipient, the better, for good or bad.

We should remain serene; calmness neutralizes thoughts and signals; thinking positive with love towards everything and everyone; without discord, without quarrels, not even the smallest one; because contradictions hinder the good waves, attracting the negative frequency; it is as simple as that.

We must learn to think positive, but we tend to fall back into bad habits, acquired since childhood by what we saw in others, and as adults, we continue with those same patterns of misbehavior, which are impregnated in us. Inadvertently our aggressiveness makes love ones suffer, often; later on, we are remorseful for accidentally, having hurt another.

We must try to eradicate these bad habits as soon as possible, in children, adults, and even in the elderly. Everything is possible when there is a will.

The ignorant disembodied spirits are pleased when finding humans to manipulate; using them for entertainment; without the person having an idea of what's happening. That's why we must throw away friction, immorality, excesses, hate; closing the doors to the energy raiders.

We must sow love and peace; care for your garden, it will give you beautiful flowers.

July 10, 2011.
(Intuition from unknown spirit.)

Enough nonsense! Earthly life is serious; a very serious thing. Permission to embody is not given easily, and in the conditions we desire, and with the ones that we have always loved, it's more difficult. All that must be combined and requested; when it is achieved it is a blessing, a gift from God.

We cannot and must not forsake life, or the importance of incarnation; it's an opportunity to grow and be charitable; it can be a huge step for the spirit, according to the knowledge acquired.

Lazy humans suffering defeat, wasting a lifetime; comprehend much later their mistakes; they cry and suffer their ignorance. We must keep the soul alert, aware of thoughts, intentions and actions; asking: can I do better? Am I fulfilling my mission?

Let's continue learning, serving, thanking our Father who forgives, by giving us another chance to restore ourselves. Love firmly, stay firm; set in your loving ways. Not *"Wishy washy"*, or timid; dare, to dream, to do! To achieve; reaching for the unknown, but the good unknown. It's there; try to reach it! Strive for the best; without arrogance, giving your best. Many surprises will come, from unexpected places.

July 18, 2011.

(Intuition from my mother Monserrate's spirit. Lake.)

There is so much natural beauty here, in small scale; there are also large, grandiose, panoramas, and it is all God. To feel peace and serenity is a reward; and doing so in the midst of so much tumult, is a blessing; searching for, it is found.

Daughter, remember that to yearn for; is power. Your books *(Memorias in English/Spanish.)* contain great teachings; with so, so, much love, in the pages; a loving testament of faith and charity; sharing love with humanity. Divine and beloved God, thank you.

August 7, 2011.
(Intuition from unknown spirit.)

What a day! What a life! Turbulent to say the least; but you've learned a lot; you have corrected several of your habits, and have amended faults; although you still have some left.

What is the right or correct thing to do? Who knows? It's all up to you. Keep on living; dealing with your duties. Praying and hoping for something better, but you don't give up; no, no, you stay on course. You know in your heart that all is well with your soul; it is a healthy soul with a good attitude. Life has not spoiled you; it has not broken your spirit, so, the best is yet to come; could be, why not?

August 12, 2011.
(Intuition from unknown spirit; elated.)

My God! Thank you! Oh, my God! We love you very much and thank you! We repeat often: *"All is not lost."* and with good reason! There is always hope in all matters; it has been proven over and over again. You see it, and live it often, sister! The unexpected happens, situations change, improving.

The Creator is Merciful, always understanding, and tolerant of our ignorant or malicious acts. Time flies! It just doesn't exist! However it sometimes seems like it doesn't move. No, no, it is happening quickly. Don't hesitate, stay focused. Finish your little book! *(This book.)* Inspiration will come!

August 23, 2011.
(Intuition from my sister Helena's spirit.)

Peace and love sister dearest; God is everything, don't forget it. Enlightenment of the soul, and of the mind for all; love unifies. As usual we are holding on to each other in an eternal embrace of happiness, of peace and solidarity. You will achieve your request; with God's permission. *(Automatic writing.)* We're ready to work.

You have so many blessings, more than you know; a time for transition, good changes happening; improving your circumstances. Keep on working with those entities that inspire you; ideas are seeds that you are planting and they will blossom.

Finish this book, it's important, it will travel farther than previous ones; pleasant surprises and a change of routine looms. Wishing all of you, peace, love, serenity, harmony and spiritual stability; all essential elements to be happy.

August 24, 2011.

(Intuition from my beloved Albert's spirit.)

Malena dearest, it's good that you are alert and excited about the writings; we will succeed, yes, yes, like Helena affirms; discipline has helped you a great deal. All is resolved with faith and patience, you will see; follow your goals, little by little, insist.

Your organism *(Body)* is solid like a rock; its faith and mind operating over matter, strengthened by breast milk. Your mother gave you many blessings; taking good care and nurturing you well.

(Below a lovely message from beloved Albert. (2008)

God is Benevolent, Merciful; allowing nonsense, knowing that whenever we desire it, we can amend our lives and find the right path. Eventually the spirit tires of suffering, and seeks peace; wanting to soar, fly; extending its *MISTICAL WINGS,* ascending; it is a peak moment.

Everyone can do it; we have the ability to climb; just by wishing, by motivating ourselves; everything depending on us. The enlightened spirits are happy seeing us making an effort. When good intentions stir, it's a call to the Universe, to God; asking for assistance and it arrives, and it doesn't fail.

August 25, 2011.

(Intuition from unknown spirit. Lake)

I like it here; the sounds of nature intoxicate; are calming and relaxing, making me dream. Our Father covers us, sending messengers to protect us; it is so, you must believe, it's very true. Have no fears, no doubts; whatever is best, will be. You've seen God's wonders with your own eyes; affairs are resolved, occurring unexpectedly; it happens when your mind is focused, and you give yourself to God; they work together. *(Prayers answered and affairs smoother.)*

August 26, 2011.

(Intuition from Gustavo's spirit.)

To my huge surprise; I received a lovely intuition related to my mother and her great love in a past life. It's a beautiful love story of a lifetime that Monserrate remembered, related, and cherished; it's included in my first book; it is precious.

The day of her passing my mother saw the great love of her prior lifetime in France; his name was Gustavo and he was a poet. He lost her too soon; she died during childbirth, along with their twins.

I received the message, read it quickly, and put it aside with other notes. I didn't notice the signature on the bottom of the page, nor did I remember having written these lines or written his name, until I reread my notes.

God had an immense surprise in store for me, because I often wondered if they were still together in the other life; until my mother told me that Gustavo was very happy, because I had included their eternal love story in my book.

The following is automatic writing:

"I have a verse for you, write: I went to visit her one lovely day. She was a rose among the roses; she was beautiful, slender and joyful; as I looked at her I couldn't believe my good fortune; I was happy knowing that I loved her and that she loved me too.

"Those are beautiful things that occur from time to time, few savoring them on earth; they are matters of the spirit; predestined encounters."

"I knew when I first saw her; knew that she was my light, my sun, moon and divine white lily.

"Today we are together; you can see that God is Wise, Generous and Just; He had it reserved for us."

"I am with her now; we kiss, embrace, and we praise; we are grateful souls, that are enjoying the eternal pure love, that we so desired."

Gustavo

August 29, 2011.

(Intuition from unknown spirit.)

We develop strength as we stumble in the dense world; we slip, fall, and pick ourselves up constantly; saved by the skin of our teeth; but God is always there, and also our brothers and sisters assisting us.

We must learn our lessons, that is true; don't be misled thinking that you can get away with murder; not ever. Go along with the flow of life; willingly, without complaining. What must be, will be. Comply, do, achieve and be thankful.

Obviously you don't see the end of the road; it's better that way; take each turn, hill, flatland in stride; skipping over the pebbles, or tossing them aside.

Advance you must; no, no stopping! Pausing yes, stopping no! The day will come when the path becomes prettier, clearer, wider, shorter and easier; you'll see, meet, rejoice with love ones; celebrating evolution, achievement, and advancement.

September 3, 2011.

(Intuition from unknown spirit.)

In the name of Almighty God; here we are again. I have a message, many messages to share with the aching world.

Listen well; it's all a great task; millions and millions of minds together, creating a large painting. All are artists with multiple colored brushes, which are their thoughts; and each applying to the canvas, his touch, his tone; some more than others, with more or less, love.

All this creates a big halo, or ring, which is a layer of energy, covering the planet; it's like putting a transparent lining on the planet. This cover made of thoughts gives the environment lightness or density, according to the thoughts and actions of each entity; converted into energy; the colors of the painters of the world. Each human bringing something to the gaseous canvas that's oscillating; energy fluctuates, and those are the emotions, thoughts and deeds of the inhabitants of the planet.

We in the spirit world contemplate all that; it is a spectacular sight, but it is also troublesome, because we can observe the large spots of dark, grey and undecipherable colors that are applied.

That mixture or swirls of colors are passions affecting the Earth and its inhabitants. The vibrant and rotating mass receives the impacts of hatred or indifference that humans congregated there exude; that's why upheavals or natural phenomena occur. If humans do not rectify their ways eradicating hatred and negative passions, this dense and hostile environment will be shaking the Earth's layers, again and again.

Our purpose is to help, guide and assist our brothers; therefore we call on them; to reflect and restraint, so that the white flag of love can finally indicate that humans have a new purpose; which is only to love each other.

September 5, 2011.

(Intuition from unknown spirit.)

Try, keep trying to write; that is the formula to reach goals. Perseverance, faith, work and love; it seems so simple, and yet so hard to achieve.

Many are distracted, entertained; just plain lazy, not wanting to be disturbed or inconvenienced. Advice, lessons, preaching, bores them What for? They ask, and repeat: *"It does no good."*

Yet, it is helpful; bad habits can be corrected, allowing new ideas to flow, thus making souls aware of new goals. With those new positive thoughts, possibilities arise, and they begin to feel complete, whole, with no voids; the emptiness is gone. Their world, as they now see, and feel it, changes for the better, because their thoughts changed; it's a new mind-set, positive reprogramming.

They had been hoping to attain the apparently unobtainable; but now, their life becomes bearable on earth, knowing, that everything is there for them; at beckon call, with their new thoughts.

May the Creative Energy embrace and engulf you in pure love and light. Oh Creator! We thank thee, always and forever.

Brothers and sisters look around you, nature has a calming effect; it is a salve that calms the soul and the body. Those tense, stressed muscles relax, the mind widens and thoughts of blissful moments rush in; good thoughts invade your mind and soul.

You are an independent and free willed soul trapped in a routine that saddens you, but be aware that it's a give and take in earthly life, an exchange; when you know and accept it with love, it becomes bearable, and even enjoyable at certain times.

Only God is perfect; all situations, circumstances on earth are imperfect, yet, it's possible to overcome the hurdles by doing our utmost.

Now you are living a moment of inspiration and communication; willing and receiving, because you are at peace and in a proper place to achieve it. We know the first steps are always slow and unsteady, but you will get ahead with much success.

September 6, 2011.

(Intuition from unknown spirit.)

The best antidote for depression is faith; it is beautiful; picking you up, from profound cliffs; faith saves you. You will always have troubles in that world; waves that one learns to ride; upheavals that fade in obscurity.

There is a bright light; and it will always be there for you, created by love, faith, lightness, peace and tranquility. We are not sure where we are going but it's a safe harbor, you know that. It is wonderful to hope, to wait, and continue with goodwill, while doing chores tastefully, and with piety; knowing everything is cause and effect. Optimistically keep going down the road carrying seeds, to plant, and later, later, to feed others.

September 9, 2011.

(Intuition from unknown spirit.)

Let me tell you a short story; it is pretty and has a lesson. Many years ago in a northern city lived a very professional and successful writer. The young man knew about the spirit world, he studied it and had much faith, but this good person was somewhat lazy, neglected his nutrition, and he also drank a lot.

Eventually he was so weak, that he had to quit his job and his mind began to fail him, because of the depressing situation that he faced. Unwittingly his fragility and addiction to alcohol made him a victim of wandering invisible entities, tormenting him with nightmares.

He was diagnosed bi-polar; medicines calmed his anxiety but he began to hallucinate, worsening his condition. The poor man suffered, but his great faith sustained him. In desperation and with great physical effort he began to pray daily, asking for assistance from enlightened spirits and particularly from his Mother.

Something wonderful happened; in a dream he saw and heard his mother saying she was happy that he prayed; that they were already helping, but not to stop asking for assistance, and to go on with his prayers for protection.

The writer stopped drinking, continuing with his prayers, with great discipline.

The nocturnal visits from unscrupulous lurking spirits gradually ceased and the nightmares were less frequent.

Confessing everything to the doctor, who luckily was also a believer; and helped him by withdrawing the strong medication; replacing it with something milder for his imbalance. The young man recovered his strength and finally returned to work, but without neglecting his prayers.

One night in his dream, his mother appeared again, telling him; *"My son, your faith has saved you. Your love of God; your discipline and your devotion have rescued you."* It happened: I was cured, thank God, I was cured, cured; my sister.

September 10, 2011.

(Intuition from unknown spirit.)

Supposedly one only knows what can be seen, but there is much more beyond the horizon; the apparent indefinite is not so imprecise, it is there plain as day for everyone to see and to learn from.

Many are nearsighted; unhappy souls brushing, and pushing against each other; in a blind stampede; never pausing to take a closer look at life and their reality. It's not so difficult to stop, look and listen attentively. The answers are there; when you focus; the picture becomes clearer with the new light that has interrupted your reverie. It is just a matter of will; wanting and doing it.

Remember what Helena said: searching while in need; you will be rewarded. Goodness is all around us, we must expand our soul and touch it; the soul needs uplifting, not downsizing.

Humans build structures; molding their lives with thoughts or with decisions, every moment; also with actions; hopefully for the better, not worse. We can make ourselves happy, enlightened and joyful, if we so desire.

Fulfilled duty is very meaningful; same on earth, as here. Peace and love, calmness, and spiritual stability, are all essential things to live well. Mercy and patience are lovely and good for the spirit; the basis for advancement and progress; nothing ends in the Universe; it's only transformation.

September 11, 2011.

(Intuition from unknown spirit.)

Love me father, love me; your dear mother, Monserrate always said that, and I repeat: love me Father, love me. Our Creator's light shines in the darkness, illuminating the path that leads to another greater light. God favors us in the negative and in the less negative matters, because everything becomes positive with the love of God, and help arrives, surely it arrives; today tomorrow and forever.

Today we ask in particular for the souls who cry out, still tied to their sad memories; may they leave behind those recollections; forgetting the gloomy picture and physical pain, there is no longer pain, only joy of God. We love you sister; hard working little ant; our work is very beautiful. Go ahead!

September 13, 2011.

(Intuition from unknown spirit.).

Let me tell you good sister that you have a great debt with God, because you have received many, many blessings in this incarnation. Yes, you have sorrows today; although small, and frustrations with an imposed routine; but your life has and has had many shades; pretty and cheerful colors, and you have enjoyed your work very much. Those are all gifts from God, and they continue; this is still another; the contact with us is definitely a blessing.

There is a reason in all this, a mission; yours and ours, merged, the same commitment: charity. There's not one single act by accident, or by chance, no! Expect more messages; yes, important ones. Continue the book with great care, review it well; but publish it. Don't drop the ball!

September 16, 2011.

(Intuition from unknown spirit.)

Light and progress; dear Gildita, here I am! Yes, shared love is beautiful and it's prettier among many souls seeking goodness to do charity; so we are. That's our spirit family, multicolored, vintage, strong roots, growing; in constant growth, without stopping; for what? Pauses, yes, selected pauses made for more resistance, that's all that's necessary.

There will be nothing ugly in your way, sister, the slits become avenues. Many think of you like an old friend; you left a loving impression on them; it is fixed in their souls. Lucky you, few achieve it.

September 17, 2011.
(Intuition from unknown spirit.)

In the name of Almighty God; let's understand the mechanisms of the spirit. It is complex, but also simple. How? I'll tell you; we will review it in parts.

First, the newly created soul is similar to a fetus; an ethereal entity composed of pure and substantial energy with spontaneous impulses, and a sleeping consciousness; gradually awakening, and taking the initiative of its actions, and little by little developing its identity, consciousness, individuality or personality as it is customary called. That consciousness or individuality is eternal, it never dies; thus taking different names in multiple incarnations but it is the same entity in a flourishing evolution; supposedly progressing.

Some are slow and left behind; others lose their way until they wish to seek the light. All this occurs at an indefinite stretch, but usually it is a long period, although in the astral plane, time is not measured like on Earth; here we measure time by the progress achieved.

The second part is circumstances, atmosphere, and proximity to entities. The spirit in its initial stages senses a Supreme Intelligence and by instinct wants to advance, progress, to seek happiness, to reach its destiny; to become part of the Creative Universal Energy which is God.

Beginning the pilgrimage in multiple areas; this entity, again instinctively; understands surroundings have an effect; impacting, influencing; supporting but it has options; ascension, or remaining stationary in ignorance.

Now considering that natural resources must be developed, in order to emerge from the labyrinth; to take flight; moving on, able to improve its spiritual conditions. It's not easy, but that's the challenge.

The developing spiritual entity learns that by overcoming obstacles, lifting stones on the road, and seeking enlightenment; spiritual growth is achieved. In its first incarnations it meets others who help or hinder him/her; that's when free will takes a greater importance; no longer a victim, it becomes its own judge and jury. We know that the Universal laws of cause and effect are always present in our evolution; results or effects always have a cause, a justification.

So here you are today; looking for the reasons and justifications for events in your life. Understand that others always influence; at least try to influence in our lives. The circumstances created by collective thoughts influence the planet, society and our lives, along with other souls who try to influence our actions, and frequently succeed.

During the sleep period we rest our vehicle, the body; escaping to get a spiritual booster, or asking for advice, or even to continue with a project that we have been working on in the astral plane. Waking up forgetting; although at times intuition or recollection remains, and it could be beneficial.

We must stay attuned and in harmony with God and the laws of the Universe, which are calming, harmonizing and energizing; arousing healthy and constructive ideas, inspiring new goals.

September 20, 2011.

(Intuition from unknown spirit.)

You all know the results of bad deeds; negative attracts negativity; it is a law of nature; part of cause and effect. Therefore think and act positively, even small actions, including gestures; avoiding malicious gestures. Surround yourselves with love, goodness; all positive elements, because it is a winning formula, it is victory over adversity.

Celebrate life when it has been an existence of service to others; that is the way to rejoice our birth or entry into this world. *(It was my birthday.)*

We all incarnate or arrive with a purpose or a mission and if we acknowledge that we have partly succeeded or if we are on the way to achieving it, then we must celebrate.

Congratulations! Our gift to you; a loving orchard of flowers with the colors of fondness, converted into kisses; that is the way we love here.

(Intuition from another unknown spirit.)

Do not believe everything that you hear or read; take from different sources and reach your own conclusions, using your common sense. On earth no one is perfectly right, we all have shortcomings and faults; thus we are here.

September 21, 2011.

(Intuition from my sister Helena's spirit.)

Peace and love sister; there is no doubt that God is so Generous, so Kind; every day we receive messages of love; resulting from past actions, yes, you left love tracks. Sometimes we have to step back to get impulse, it is a necessary thrust.

What you are doing with the little book is good; take care of it; very soon it will be out to the world. What is happening is wonderful; we assure you beautiful things, rewards for your actions. You are advancing in great strides with the messages, they're authentic, real; it is a combination; a union of souls, with a great desire to serve. You asked for it and they have responded.

The messages will continue arriving, it will be much better when you establish a routine; that's about to happen. There is willingness from all, with God's blessing. This book which you are preparing will be widely read, previous ones were pathfinders; you planted and cultivated the ground. There are those looking for your work, you have followers.

September 26, 2011.

(Intuition from unknown spirit.)

Yes, it's me! Always ready! Listen and write. Not a leaf moves without God's will; you know that well, your mother always repeated it.

Now you're watching it, close up. Your life has been a great lesson, because of faults that you had to correct; with many shortcomings of your overly conceited spirit; not sins, faults.

Present circumstances to purge; to detoxify your excess pride, were your choice. You see; you have captured a clear image of the picture that we wanted to present; you're an example of what can be achieved when there is disposition. A great desire to grow, to serve, moves you, that is your motivation. No need to doubt, to fear, or search; everything is clear; you selected; God approved.

You came with the support of your mother, and other enlightened and loving entities. Now you have time to elaborate further, and will do it. When you come to our world, you'll be very happy, satisfied and buoyant! Progress you were looking for, progress you will have.

September 28, 2011.

(Intuition from unknown spirit.)

Peace, love, enlightenment, progress, beloved sister; today as yesterday you're a believer; same disciplinary and loving entity, but those are virtues; faults can be corrected, forgotten, and erased from this episode of life. The important thing is to want to *"Delete faults"* wanting to do it, is powerful.

God sends messengers; there is always divine assistance available. It is lovely to wait every day for surprises that are God's gifts. You know that they will come and you get excited waiting for them. They come in different wrappers, large or small; they are *"Kisses from God",* as your mother still says.

It's been five and a half years since Monserrate came to our spirit world, it's incredible! Contact has not been interrupted; we are even more bonded. Enlightenment is coming Gilda, lots of light, joy, space, yes, wait for it. You will be a great medium!

September 29, 2011.

(Intuition from unknown spirit.)

It's me! As your brother Nel says, God bless him; he's a man of peace and with great love for the world. We are all different, but equal in God's love; that unifies us, all led by His Powerful Hand.

Yes, you constantly have our inspiration; it is a mutual goal. You have no idea, how you benefited; yes, with your prayers you have cleanse your soul with Mint. A voluntary preparation; mutual agreement to attain a goal; a huge mission of peace and love for humanity.

These are issues difficult to explain because they have so many details, of many proportions. We must stimulate others; encourage them to continue, to achieve goals. Their successes are our successes because we are all one.

We are one! It's so hard to believe; isn't true? We are unique, but the same; How is that? Yes, it's true, each one is an individual piece, but each piece is part of a bigger piece; Glorious! Magnificent! God, Universal Consciousness.

That's why we must love our brothers; by loving ourselves, by loving you, you love them all.

September 30, 2011.

(Intuition from unknown spirit.) (Lake)

In the name of Almighty God; look at the ducklings by your side, sitting at your feet; they have peace, are confident, at ease with your company. They sense a pleasant frequency; you're a friend, they feel that you will not harm them.

Every earth being senses or captures vibrations from others or from places; frequencies transmitted by thoughts, signals that we exchange consistently, and they rebound; what we send, we receive.

Humans self-punish in accordance with their intentions, and actions; therefore you must watch your thoughts; maintaining harmony, peace and love in the environment; we create daily circumstances.

Sister, do not waste these lovely moments; enjoy nature; engulf yourself in the sun, the breeze, everything that surrounds you, even the ducklings; charging you up, with pure energy, although minor.

October 26, 2011.
(Intuition from unknown spirit.)

In the name of Almighty God; you already know me; it's good that we are in sync. Gilda, don't see the limitations, look at the opportunities, which are many, many and all depend on us. You have to keep your peace and your calm in order to think and be ready to work. There is nothing more essential and clear than that.

God is always available; 24/7, His messengers respond immediately; *"Spirit Rescue Unit."*

You simply have to hold the reins well, and go on with goodwill and love; hoping to serve.

Woe to the poor, the rich, poor! Without peace, without love, faith, or hope, they are destitute. Not *"Homeless", "Soul-less."* Empty minds and spirits; with pessimistic attitudes; the living dead.

Our Creator has wayward children; but, He does not forsake them; knowing that somehow He will put them back on track; reaching them with His love, as a good Father does; loving them and caring about their well-being and happiness.

Here we go! We're all part of that rescue team. Our sights are placed, fixed; on supporting them, alleviating and guiding them; that is our goal.

How? With inspirations, ideas, and messages; manifestations of Divine Love, which they perceive daily, seeing it in their lives; compelling them to think, reflect; and make transcendental decisions. You're part of our team; a small auxiliary. Keep on loving and working sister; the task is beautiful.

October 27, 2011.

(Intuition from unknown spirit.)

In the name of Almighty God; *"Life is a dream,"* they say, I say no; life is often a nightmare; but we can wake up and turn it into a beautiful dream. How is that? It's not so difficult. While your body sleeps, your spirit rises elsewhere, leaving your body resting.

Your soul is jubilant having a free moment, it roams, encountering loved ones, sharing, learning with them; making good use of this period in the astral world.

Without being asleep you can learn to detach; spiritualize, feeling buoyant, agile and in peace.

With the power of thought you can achieve it; cultivating loving, positive, constructive thoughts; reprogramming as they say now.

In such a state of wakefulness, but with the mind and spirit serene, you can see life through spiritual lens; focusing on what is really worthwhile, what is truly real, and throwing aside what is insignificant, all the rubbish polluting your mind and your body. Do not waste time on nonsense and gibberish.

Thinking with faith it's always positive because you dream awake. Thus, you have *"Life is a dream."*

October 31, 2011.

(Intuition from unknown spirit.

Love Gilda, love the world; love your work and your destiny. Yes, the book has so much love; you should be proud, I am too; I am **Gabriel!**

You are surprised! Yes, Gilda, it's a wonderful surprise, for me too! I didn't know if I could reach you, but God knows best.

He knows when it's the precise time. It is said that the student meets the teacher, when the time is right.

We have much to talk; tomorrow will be great, in many ways.

*(This entity signed his name in large script by automatic writing: **GABRIEL**)*

(I had heard Pio Gabriel a few times through my mother, Monserrate. He is so wise and his messages magnificent; I included them in both my prior books. Below an inspirational message from Pio Gabriel; July 14, 2005.)

Spirit of Pio Gabriel:

On a daily basis think and repeat. Have I learned something today? Did I make good use of my life? It's not easy but it should be asked and could be obtained. As time goes by, none of us worry too much about taking advantage of our lives; but every day there is a surprise, and it can be a pretty one.

One can feel ecstasy by throwing away the rubbish from the road; it's like receiving a spiritual cleansing. We are capricious; falling on our knees and hurting ourselves, but we shouldn't fall, it hurts, and the pain restrains us; we break down and do not know what to do, nevertheless; God asks for so little.

If you're programmed you can see the path that's ready for you, that you have reached, to pass through. At times it's unclear and it's our own fault by not wanting to think; by mundane entanglements. Life is pretty; it's not ugly; it can be clean, allowing us to develop; thank you God, for loving us.

He chooses His favorite friends; those that want to reach Him with devotion.

We must be fair with God because He gives us a weightless life, but we are arrogant, too conceited;

with so many defects. We toss it away; that happens to the know it all; they are so small and they receive exactly what they deserve.

We need education no matter our knowledge; God always knows more than you, conceited one; for that reason you limp, but God in His Benevolence gives us a crutch, so as not to limp. He loves us, embracing us; we're fragile, selfish and whimsical; the laziness is so great, that we do not want to think; but even then, God leads us on the right path, loving us; always giving us a hand.

Gilda you're a fortunate soul; you're touched by the spirits that love you and that nobody sees. You must say: "Praise God that I do this because I feel it."

Your mother is the one soul that has loved you the most in this lifetime; Helena and your brother too.

Thank God that you published those books with your courage; because "Without money, no honey" You're strong, laborious; a kind soul; yielding your place to others. In you there is a very beautiful thing; your love for family, and for the spiritual entities.

Occasionally we think about the heavy loads that we pick up along the road, and we say: "I have learned greatly from that journey." At that very moment you're making a commitment to God. telling him: "Help me; help me to take the right path," If you say it with faith, sincerely feeling it, because of your past experiences; look, it's as if a light has been lit in your spiritual evolution; you will achieve it; you can achieve it. How wonderful it is to be able to reach a high degree of advancement for your soul.

One must be thankful and committed, and all the commitments must be met. We must always be strong and determined; because when we have a commitment with God; with the most Supreme and these good allies, good souls that come to visit; one must comply. The benevolent entities have been very noble; they took care of their harvest, their orchards, their planting, and of their dear ones. I tell you that they used their immense faith and love of God; they never stopped, because of laziness; they continued with the sincere oaths of a true challenge, of a divine symbol that was a gift from the Supreme; and they were tireless.

As you can see, your good sister of past lives Helena, compels you to go on sowing orchards; it is because she knows that you do not lack anything, that you have an excess of many things because she knows you; living with you previously, twice very close to you. She achieved many things, and she knows that you pursue tranquility, wellbeing and supreme happiness; those are only achieved when one has a commitment with the Creator. You have struggled very much spiritually; that's why she tells you: "Forward, good soul, dear sister; in the past you have known how to stop to look and to choose what is worthwhile."

GABRIEL

November 3, 2011.

(Intuition from Gabriel's spirit.) (My mind wondered)

In the name of Almighty God: did you think that our communication would cease? No, impossible, we have so, so, much to talk about. There's a great deal of agitation confusing your thoughts, but that's part of life's charm; the salt and pepper; keep going.

Spirits transport by thoughts; accommodating to different obstacles and environments; but there are no barriers for us. No matter where or how, we are always here; it's a wonderful, magnificent, moment of illumination and agility; not all succeed of course; it also depends on their development and their level of evolution.

It is a heartrending sensation of emotions; joy, surprise, curiosity, visits to love ones, collaboration between friends; sadness; seeing mundane scenes.

(Bird sings) What a better way to meditate, than listening to a bird singing, his song makes us happy and helps us to detach ourselves from the routine.

November 5, 2011.

(Intuition from Gabriel's spirit.)

In the name of Almighty God; here we are again. What bliss to fly, like a bird; we the spirits can fly that way, with our invisible wings, our ***mystical wings***.

It's good that you are looking for peace; it is so helpful. Tranquility and serenity numbs us; we float, disengaging. Keep practicing your automatic writing; you achieved it; left it because of circumstances; you will accomplish it again.

November 6, 2011.

(Intuition from Gabriel's spirit.)

In the name of Almighty God; we are here, close by; some far away but standing by; they are aware, in the know. Yes you must get on with the book, there is much more to do; go on sister, continue to grow, recording, writing, taking notes and depositing them. You are well on your path, "*On track.*" It's a matter of finishing the book. Love you.

November 10, 2011.

(Intuition from Gabriel's spirit.)

In the name of Almighty God; it's good and positive to learn. There are always lessons; I don't mean in school or educational institutions; I mean lessons in daily life. There's always something to learn, pausing to contemplate, reflect, analyze and retain details; they can be beautiful or not, but you always learn something. We are enriched when we stop in our fast march.

Yes, yes, it's me, Gabriel; it's lovely, lovely, what is happening; a union of thoughts from devoted souls, with a same ideal or goal, loving each other. What you asked for is being given to you, in part.

(Asked to receive all messages from the entities by automatic writing.) The ideal moment will come; it will be automatic, without your mind interfering.

*(He signed a **G**.)*

November 22, 2011.

(Intuition from Gabriel's spirit.)

In the name of Almighty God, listen well Gilda; we are convinced that soon you will be able to see us, get ready. It will be a shock at first, because of the surprise and joy; when it passes you will rejoice; because you have achieved one more step, one more step, towards advancement. *(I wondered if it was time to suspend the intuitions and finish the book, with what I had up to date).*

You will know when to take a pause; stay calm, do not lose your good sense and rhythm; everything is going well.

November 29, 2011.

(Yesterday Gabriel told me, that in a day or so, he would dictate the last page. Today I woke up late and expected a visit; so I rushed in order not to be interrupted. Lighting my candle and starting to pray, I heard; "In the name of Almighty God." Thinking it was my restless mind; I went back to my prayer, heard again; "In the name of Almighty God" I knew that Gabriel had a message for me, so I went to the desk to write.

(Intuition from Gabriel's spirit)

You heard my signal well, that means you're very receptive. Dearest and loving sister, everything comes to an end apparently, but they're only cycles; nothing ends in the Universe, as we have repeated.

Stay calm; it helps you, and us. You know very well that several projects must be completed; there's no reason to doubt, everything is a reality; that is the honest truth. You've worked very well, and the book will be ready soon. Thanks for being available and for your commendable love.

Live your life fulfilling the duties which God gave you; that's your task for today; and you must deliver the completed test in order to pass the subject.

Let's not miss this opportunity to thank all the spiritual entities who collaborated in various forms, in our project; a large group of spirits with lights; each one with a lamp, seeking to illuminate the world.

We are unified, with a great commitment and mission; wishing to leave our legacy of love and peace in these pages, so that everyone can satisfy their cravings and worldly anxieties, and therefore be able to climb the mountain of faith, hope, and brotherly love; working for peace on earth.

Each one of us, and we are many; will provide vibrations of light; illuminating each reader while they stop to browse these pages. We hope to leave in their souls, seeds; golden by God's sun, illuminated by God's stars, radiant with God's charity; our gift.